COUNTRY HOUSE SECRETS

BEHIND CLOSED DOORS

RUTH BINNEY

FOREWORD BY

JULIAN FELLOWES

CREATOR OF

DOWNTON ABBEY

RP

RYDON
PUBLISHING

A Rydon Publishing Book
35 The Quadrant
Hassocks
West Sussex
BN6 8BP
www.rydonpublishing.co.uk
www.rydonpublishing.com

First published by Rydon Publishing in 2019
Copyright © Ruth Binney 2012, 2019
The majority of the text in this book has been previously published in *Wise Words
& Country House Ways*, published by David & Charles in 2012.

A CIP catalogue record for this book is available from the British Library.
ISBN: 978-1-910821-31-2

Printed in Poland by BZ Graf

CONTENTS

FOREWORD BY
JULIAN FELLOWES CREATOR OF *DOWNTON ABBEY*

Other nations may have supportable claims to lead in the fields of food or fashion or modern technology, but no one could seriously challenge the British when it comes to life in a country house. The great house, with its gardens and dependencies, with its park and farmland, its stables and carpentry shops and kitchen and fisheries, was a kingdom in itself, and if not quite self-supporting, it was often almost so. Perhaps it is this sense of completeness, a world sufficient unto itself, that explains the continuing fascination with all that the English country house represents.

It was an arrangement that involved men and women from every background who each had a crucial role to play in this complex machine. In fact, one of the most pleasing of recent development in our appreciation of the country house is that we have begun to see that these places were part of our shared history and not simply the homes of the upper classes.

When I was young there was a tendency, with any house in the care of the National Trust or opened by its owners, to put only the public rooms on display for the ticket buyers to marvel at. And they were very impressive, those drawing rooms, libraries and gilded ballrooms, but there was no sign of the kitchens or work

places, thereby denying the visitor any
real sense of how it worked. One of
the first houses to break with this rule
was Lanhydrock, in Cornwall. A fire in
the 1880s had destroyed much of the
original and the rebuild had resulted
in a series of reception rooms designed
according to the not very inspiring standards of the late 19th
century, but, by contrast, the state-of-the-art kitchens, the
pantries, the brushing and ironing and lamp rooms could
not have been more interesting. The National Trust then
commendably decided to make it a priority to open these
places and, for once, to give the public a real idea of the
beehive nature of a great house, where the work rooms were
intimately linked to the lives of the family in a continuous
cycle of labour, in which no detail was too small not to be
governed by rules and custom and etiquette and costume.

This is the world which Ruth Binney has brought so
wonderfully to life in her book. To a modern eye, there
was certainly a good deal of unfairness involved in the
arrangement, there is no point in pretending otherwise,
but there was also a level of dedication and skill and, above
all, commitment, from both groups, the family and their
servants, that seems so admirable, especially when viewed
from our rather selfish and undisciplined century. I do not
believe that we should be too nostalgic for the ways that are
gone, but, by the same token, nor do I believe we should be
too afraid of learning from their example.

INTRODUCTION

Simulated hugely by the award-winning *Downton Abbey* created by Julian Fellowes, who has so kindly contributed the foreword to this book, interest in the British country house has never been stronger. Now *Country House Secrets*, which concentrates largely on life in the Georgian, Victorian and Edwardian eras, takes you behind closed doors to reveal the life and workings of the country house both above and below stairs, starting from the contemporary maxims used to advise and inform the members of the household and their guests about every aspect of daily life.

Details of the way in which the virtually self-sufficient country house worked day to day is reflected in each of the book's six chapters, beginning with 'Keeping House' and progressing to 'The Daily Routine' and 'The Country House Kitchen'. Since correct behaviour was so important to all activities of the house, 'A Matter of Manners' addresses the essentials of etiquette, a theme that also extends into 'Leisure, Entertainment and Sport', whether this was hunting, fishing or attending a ball or country house wedding. Finally, 'Garden and Grounds' focuses on everything from the cultivation of exotic fruit for the table to the importance of the dovecote, ice house and stables.

Whenever possible, information for the book has come from contemporary sources, of which the most significant are listed at the back of the book. Any of the 'recipes' included,

whether for food or cleaning materials, have not been tested
– they are here for interest alone and, if used, are entirely at
the reader's own risk.

Without the resources of The London Library, and the
many volumes loaned by friends and family, the intriguing
experience of researching and writing this book would
have been impossible, and I thank them all for their help
and support. I am also indebted to Julian Fellowes for his
foreword, my publisher Robert Ertle, editor Verity Graves-
Morris, designer Prudence Rogers and the team at Rydon
Publishing, for their care and enthusiasm in the creation of
this edition, and to Stephen and Caroline Jaques for their
help in sourcing the illustrations.

Ruth Binney
Yeovil, Somerset, 2019

KEEPING HOUSE

Managing any country house, whether inherited or purchased, was a huge task. Keeping it running well not only demanded considerable resources but also the necessary skill to hire, employ and keep happy, healthy and well fed a veritable army of staff. The house needed to be properly furnished and decorated, kept up to date with the latest advances, and be warm, comfortable and clean for everyone living in it. The finances of a well-run house were always a top priority. Not only were precise records of all expenditure necessary, but they needed to be examined regularly to make sure that no fraud was being committed.

A pattern of rooms

The way the typical country house was designed, organized and arranged followed a definite pattern, with an impressive hall, drawing and dining rooms and staff quarters separated from those of the family and, by Victorian times, ostensibly invisible. The master and mistress would have their own 'apartments', often with separate bedrooms, and rooms or suites set aside for key family members and for visitors – who might even include royalty. Senior staff would have their own rooms, but juniors were accommodated in shared rooms or dormitories.

Advances in technology

The arrival of flushing lavatories and bathrooms with running water did much to improve the comfort of the country house which, before central heating, would have open fires in all family rooms in use during the winter, or on any day of the year deemed cold enough. Equally, the installation of electricity, although it caused initial anxieties, revolutionized lighting and stimulated gadget development, while the telephone provided speedy contact with the outside world.

THE HEAD OF THE HOUSEHOLD IS MASTER OF HIS REALM

WITH THE HELP OF HIS FAMILY AND SERVANTS, THE MASTER WAS OBLIGED TO ENSURE THAT BOTH THE HOUSE AND ESTATE WERE RUN WITH SEAMLESS EFFICIENCY.

As head of the family, the master of the country house was entitled to the obedience of everyone in it, including his wife and children. In return for their employment he demanded absolute loyalty from his servants, down to the lowliest scullery maid or hall boy. He could chastise, encourage or reward them according to their performance – and his own whims. But of all the virtues in his servants, loyalty and discretion were considered the most important. Without them there was a grave risk of dishonour being brought on the household.

Fair treatment was the obligation of the master to his servants, including rewards for good service, although he could in fact behave exactly as he wished. He was expected to see that they were well fed and housed, kept healthy and, if necessary, to intervene on their behalf if they ran into trouble. Once long-term, elderly servants reached retirement age he was expected to provide them with an annuity of some kind for the rest of their lives.

FOR HIMSELF AND HIS STAFF

The 18th-century diarist Charles Greville recorded that: *'The Duke of Rutland is as selfish a man as any of his class – that is, he never does what he does not like, and spends his whole life in a round of such pleasures as suit his taste, but he is neither a foolish nor a bad man, and partly from a sense of duty, partly from inclination, he devotes time and labour to the interest and welfare of the people who live and labour on his estate.'*

The yearly round

When the master of the house also conducted business in London, or served in the armed forces, the family would remain in the country for most of the year, going 'up to town' only for the London season during the summer months. Families that kept both town and country houses customarily moved from one to the other at weekends.

GOOD TEMPER SHOULD BE CULTIVATED BY EVERY MISTRESS

ONE OF THE MANY MAXIMS OF MRS BEETON AND ONE ADHERED TO BY THE BEST MISTRESSES OF COUNTRY ESTABLISHMENTS TO HELP ENSURE THAT ALL RAN SMOOTHLY.

Up to the 20th century, the number of people serving in a country house could total several dozen or more. Although the major task of the head housekeeper was to ensure that all domestic work was completed well, and in a timely manner, the ultimate responsibility lay with the mistress of the house whose attitude could have a great impact. The servants managed personally and directly by her included her lady's maid, the nurse, governess and, critically, the cook.

KEEPING STAFF HAPPY

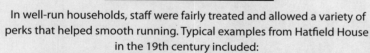

In well-run households, staff were fairly treated and allowed a variety of perks that helped smooth running. Typical examples from Hatfield House in the 19th century included:

- **For each manservant:** a pint of beer (home brewed) at lunch dinner and supper.
- **For each women servant**: a pint of the same beer at lunch and supper.
- **Cook:** the right to bones and dripping, which could be used or sold.
- **Lady's maid:** cast off clothes and accessories.
- **Butler:** candle ends and empty bottles, free to be sold.
- **Coachman:** wheels from carriages, but allowed only if the servant had been in service for more years than the age of the wheels.

As well as their physical welfare, good country house mistresses took on responsibility for the morals of her staff. At Holkham Hall in Norfolk, for instance, servants were forbidden to gamble, swear or be seen out of the village after dark. On a somewhat lighter note, maids were banned from using curl-papers in their hair (these being regarded as a total frivolity) and discouraged from dressing, when off duty, in any but the plainest clothes. Sunday church attendance was, of course, vigorously encouraged if not compulsory.

ADDITIONAL ADVICE

Expanding on her Headline advice Mrs Beeton continued '... *as upon it the welfare of the household may be said to turn; indeed, its influence can hardly be over-estimated, as it has the effect of moulding the characters of those around her, and of acting beneficially on the happiness of the domestic circle. Every head of a household should strive to be cheerful and should never fail to show a deep interest in all that appertains to the well-being of those who claim protection of her roof.'*

THE OFFICE OF HOUSE STEWARD IS OF SUPREME IMPORTANCE

IN LARGE COUNTRY HOUSES THE STEWARD WAS THE HEAD OF THE STAFF. HE NEEDED TO BE LOYAL AND HIGHLY VERSATILE.

In addition, a good steward was trustworthy and a man of manners au fait with everything from accounting to the nuances of etiquette. His chief duties were the management and hiring of staff (except for personal servants) and the economy of the household. The steward had his own room and the dedicated service of one or more men or boys. The footmen would also attend to his needs.

Accurate accounts

Keeping exact double entry accounts was a vital role of the house steward, recording the exact amounts spent and received, and the balance belonging to his employer. He needed to work with the housekeeper to ensure that all provisions brought into the house were up to quality and the bills for them checked and paid.

HIS 'JOB DESCRIPTION'

As *The Country Gentleman's Vademecum* of 1699 underlines, the steward must: *'... receive and pay all Monies, buy in the Provision for the Family, hire all Livery-men, buy all Liveries, pay all Wages... to be at his Master's Elbow during Dinner, and receive all Orders from him relating to Government; to oversee and direct the Baliff, Gardener, &c. in their Business; and also the Clerk of the Kitchen Cook, Butler &c. to whom he delivers the Provision, Wine, Beer, &c. who give him an Account of the spending it, weekly or otherwise.'*

LIVERY IS PARTICULAR TO EVERY HOUSEHOLD

THE FORMAL 'UNIFORM' FOR SOME MALE SERVANTS, LIVERY
REFLECTED GREATLY ON THE WEALTH AND POSITION OF
THE FAMILY IN WHICH THEY WERE EMPLOYED.

Livery was invariably worn by those country house
servants most on display, particularly footmen of all
ranks. The youngest liveried servants were the 'tigers', small
boys who perched on the backs of carriages or who stood on
a platform at the rear. All liveries belonged to the master,

not the servant. Daytime liveries were usually given to servants twice a year, in spring and autumn, evening ones annually. When a servant left the household the livery always had to be returned.

The colour and design of liveries were exclusive to each household, allowing families to pick out their own servants in a crowd. Blue coats, for instance formed the livery of Lord Leicester, while those of the Marquis of Bath at Longleat were mustard yellow. Buttons were silver or gold. The traditional pattern of the waistcoat, often trimmed with gold braid, was horizontal stripes. Silk stockings, and shoes with silver buckles were also *de rigeur*.

LIVERY ON THE MOVE

Coachmen also wore livery, although of a different style to that of footmen. Until the end of the 19th century, when carriages were replaced with motor cars, their dress included black boots with white tops, red or other brightly coloured greatcoats resplendent with brass buttons bearing the family crest, and hats with feathered cockades.

DRESSING FOR THE HAIR

For evenings, as well as donning white ties, liveried footmen might be required to powder their hair. To do this they dipped their heads in water, rubbed in soap to create a lather, combed it through, then applied powder from a powder puff – either a specially prepared coloured powder (violet was common) or ordinary flour. They then had somehow to manage to spend an entire evening in service without letting any powder fall onto their jackets, a feat that involved standing very still for long periods.

A HOUSEKEEPING ACCOUNT BOOK MUST INVARIABLY BE KEPT

AN ABSOLUTE ESSENTIAL OF RUNNING A COUNTRY HOUSE, AND THE DAILY RESPONSIBILITY OF THE HOUSEKEEPER IN COLLABORATION WITH THE HOUSE STEWARD.

Punctually and precisely, the housekeeper needed to record in a meticulous daily diary all the amounts paid out on that day, however small. Everything coming into the house was checked immediately by the housekeeper, not only for its quality but 'to see that in weight and measure they agree with the tickets sent with them'. Only then could they be allocated for use. Then, at the end of the month, advised Mrs Beeton, she should '… let these payments be ranged under their specific heads of Butcher, Baker, &c.; and thus will be seen the proportions paid to each tradesman…'

In houses where there was a house steward, the bills would be examined and paid by him. However the housekeeper still needed to keep a daily eye on the larder, in collaboration with the cook, so that everything necessary could be obtained, particularly when visitors were due. 'The best and most economical way possible for marketing' said *The Complete Servant*, 'is to pay ready money for all that you can, especially for miscellaneous articles, and to deal for the rest with the most respectable tradesmen.'

ADVICE FOR THE HOUSEKEEPER

Mrs Beeton advises that when '… *a housekeeper is kept, it will be advisable for the mistress to examine her accounts regularly. Then any increase of expenditure which may be apparent, can easily be explained, and the housekeeper will have the satisfaction of knowing whether her efforts to manage her department well and economically, have been successful.*'

EVERY HALL SHOULD BE DESIGNED TO IMPRESS

THE TYPICAL COUNTRY HOUSE HAD HALLS OF TWO
KINDS – ONE FOR THE FAMILY AND THEIR GUESTS, THE
OTHER FOR THEIR SERVANTS.

The hall began life in the medieval country house as a space where everyone in the household ate their meals, with the lord and his family placed on a raised dais – a kind of 'high table'. Other diners, including servants, were then arranged below them by status. Adjacent to the hall were the private chambers of the lord, his wife and family, while adjoining at the opposite end were the kitchens.

Decorum in the servants' hall

As elsewhere in the house there were strict rules of conduct in the servants' hall, as *The Complete Servant* explains:

- The housekeeper sits at the head of the table, with the cook on her right and the lady's maid on her left.
- The butler sits at the opposite end with the under butler on his right and the coachman on his left.
- The dinner is set on the table by the cook, and the beer is drawn by the under butler.
- Servants of coarse manners, vulgar habits, or profane discourse and malicious dispositions, are shunned by others and never make good their footing in first-rate families.

Musicians' galleries

As country house architecture developed, rooms were built above the hall. Galleries constructed around it were ideal for musicians, who would play during dinner and for dancing and other entertainments. Not until the 17th century did servants begin eating in their own separate hall – the first step in the gradual transformation of the country house hall into a grand entrance that could also be used for games such as billiards, and as a ballroom. Key to this change was the architect Inigo Jones who, inspired by Italian villas, added the dining saloon to country houses.

The Victorian country house hall could be exceedingly gloomy. Often designed in Gothic revival style it was invariably hung with everything from weapons to the mounted heads of stags and other creatures.

SERVANTS' QUARTERS

As it developed, the servants' hall became a little self-contained world in which passions, tempers, vices and virtues were all brought into play, and contributed to promoting welfare and happiness in the household. Commenting on the ideal arrangement of the Victorian house, *Our Homes and How to Make Them Healthy* said: *'The servants' hall should be placed within easy access of the entrance hall, and also close to the servants' entrance, so that it may be used as a waiting room when occasion demands .... The windows should so contrive that, while they should not overlook the private grounds, they should yet afford a cheerful and pleasant outlook onto the kitchen yard or the garden.'*

THE DRAWING ROOM ALLOWS FOR QUIET AND SEPARATION

THAT IS OF LADIES FROM MEN. AS IT EVOLVED THE COUNTRY HOUSE DRAWING ROOM BECAME AN INCREASINGLY ELABORATE SHOWCASE FOR WORLDLY GOODS.

The drawing room, or properly the 'withdrawing' room, began as an attachment to the bedroom then later, downstairs, as a room where people assembled before dinner and afterwards, waiting if necessary while the dinner table was being cleared. From this it developed into a public room in which visitors could also be entertained during the afternoon. For comfort, the grand Regency drawing room was furnished with a 'sofa table', a low table with flaps on each of its ends, combined with a sofa on which a lady could recline with ease. Rosewood was a favourite material, as for other furniture of the period, particularly chairs. Music was customarily played in the drawing room on a harpsichord – replaced later by the grand piano – and possibly with other instruments such as a harp and a cello.

Relaxing in splendour

Two of the many country house drawing rooms of note include:

Ham House, Surrey: North drawing room, with baroque chimney piece with cherubs and fine tapestries based on paintings of the seasons by the Flemish artist David Teniers.

Syon House, Greater London: Crimson drawing room with damask hangings and ceiling ornamented with squares and octagons each enclosing a painted panel by Angelica Kaufmann. Carpet of red, gold and blue woven especially for the room.

THE VICTORIAN DRAWING ROOM

By the Victorian era the country house drawing room had become full of furniture, as the garden designer J.C. Loudon describes: *'A large round table is usually placed in the middle of the drawing-room, on which are generally books of prints and other things to amuse the company .... Two card tables would stand one on each side of the fireplace: and, besides all these, we must have tables of various sizes, some small ones on pillars; a chess table, with an inlaid marble top, the men placed upon it; a large china dish set in a gilt sort of tripod; a sort of table flower-stand; and I cannot tell what besides .... Writing, work, and drawing boxes of handsome kinds and everything amusing, curious, or ornamental, is in its place in the drawing-room; but the host of trumpery toys so often seen there would be unworthy of a place in a room like this.'*

SMOKING AND BILLIARD ROOMS ARE CONVENIENTLY PLACED SIDE BY SIDE

BECAUSE SMOKING AND BILLIARDS WERE OFTEN COMBINED, IT WAS LOGICAL TO HAVE THE TWO ADJACENT TO EACH OTHER, OR AS ONE. LARGELY MALE PRESERVES, BOTH COULD BE ELABORATELY DECORATED.

The fashion for smoking in country houses, and its acceptability, waxed and waned over the centuries. In the late 17th century and through the 18th, smoking rooms or parlours, where pipes were enjoyed by men, particularly after dinner, were set aside in houses such as Charborough in Dorset, Kedleston Hall in Derbyshire and Lillingstone Lovell in Buckinghamshire.

From the beginning of the 1800s, however, smoking became generally less acceptable, although cigars were

SET ASIDE FOR SMOKING

Remarking on the trend in 1864, the Scottish architect Robert Kerr wrote of the '... *pitiable resources to which some gentlemen are driven, even in their own houses in order to be able to enjoy the pestiferous luxury of a cigar'* **and that these** *'have given rise to the occasional introduction of an apartment specially dedicated to the use of Tobacco.'*

still offered following dinner and smoked by men in the dining room. Only from the mid-19th century did smoking rooms become the norm and were particularly appreciated by bachelors who spent much time in country houses when not at their London clubs.

Styles of adornment

A popular style of decoration for the Victorian billiard room, which was also used by women, was to have stags' heads, plus horse portraits, or pictures with similar sporting themes, on the walls around which were raised leather benches for spectators. A high leather stool was provided for the 'nipper' who would keep the scores. Walls might also be wood panelled.

A magnificent summer smoking room in the Moorish style was created on two floors in Cardiff Castle, complete with mythological scenes based on cartoons by the imaginative

architect William Burges. The floor tiling depicted a map of the world surrounded by circles of huntsmen, horses, ships and even spouting whales, plus the globes of the medieval universe.

THE TASK OF WARMING A BIG HOUSE IS A LARGE ONE

INDEED IT WAS, ESPECIALLY IN THE DEPTHS OF WINTER, AND REMAINED SO, EVEN WITH ADVANCES IN CENTRAL HEATING.

Until the 19th century – and often into the 20th – the only means of heating a country house was the open fire. Every room, including bedrooms (although not necessarily those occupied by servants), was fitted with fireplaces, which needed constant attention and daily cleaning if they were to keep alight. It was also vital for there to be a draught, which was only too regularly supplied by cold air being sucked in through ill-fitting doors and windows. Equally, smoke often billowed out into the rooms from the downdraught created through large, wide chimneys.

The luxury of warmth

Hot air heating systems were also developed, such as the device advertised by one William Day of Lambeth in 1754 'which rarifies cold air until it is hot, and conveys it into Gentlemen's libraries and grand rooms'. At Woburn Abbey such a system was used in the early 19th century, allowing residents and guests the winter-time luxury of strolling from room to room without freezing. Radiators, as we know them today, were also a 19th century innovation. Among the first were those installed for the Duke of Wellington at Stratfield Saye in Hampshire.

MANY ADVANTAGES
One of the greatest advantages of the Rumford stove was that it helped to prevent kitchen smells from permeating the rest of the house. In newly built houses of the Victorian era it allowed the kitchen to be placed much nearer to the dining room, making it much easier to serve food piping hot.

Innovative advances

In an attempt to improve the efficiency of open fires Count Rumford (Sir Benjamin Thompson) discovered that restricting the chimney opening had the effect of increasing the updraught. By inserting bricks into the hearth to make the side walls angled, and adding a choke to the chimney to increase the speed of air going up the flue, he not only made the fire more efficient but encouraged smoke to go up the chimney. Such stoves were adapted for use in the kitchen, where they became most popular, but open fires persisted elsewhere.

THE INSTALLATION OF BATHROOMS AND WATER CLOSETS CAN IMPROVE SANITATION SIGNIFICANTLY

COUNTRY HOUSES WERE GENERALLY SLOW TO INSTALL IMPROVED INDOOR FACILITIES, BUT HOUSES SUCH AS CHATSWORTH IN DERBYSHIRE WERE IN THE FOREFRONT OF TECHNOLOGY.

By 1695 Chatsworth had at least ten water closets, made of cedar with alabaster bowls and brass fittings. They were well ahead of their counterparts – some country houses were still using earth privies even a century later. When, in the late 17th century, cold baths became fashionable many houses built bath houses in the grounds in addition to the indoor plunge baths. The bath itself might be enclosed in a building of some kind, placed in a grotto or simply be out in the open air like a swimming pool.

Bathing in privacy

For bathing, portable hip and sponge baths were used before improvements in plumbing made indoor bathrooms a practical possibility. At Carshalton House in Surrey, completed in 1720, the tiled bathroom (along with an orangery and greenhouse) was placed adjacent to an engine room for heating the water, while at Blenheim in Oxfordshire a bathroom with hot and cold running water was installed directly below the Duchess of Marlborough's bedroom and joined to it by a discreet staircase. The Duke, meanwhile, had his own ornately decorated water closet alongside his dressing room with marble floor and walls and a gilded ceiling.

Innovation and improvement

With advances in Victorian technology, bathrooms and water closets became much easier to install. New houses such as Bearwood in Berkshire, begun in the 1860s, had no less than 22 water closets and 5 bathrooms, with water pumped from an engine house in the kitchen court to the top of a water tower in the garden. Equally, older houses were greatly improved, as at Cardiff Castle, where the Roman marble bath, inlaid with fishes, newts and an octopus made in metal, was converted to use running water.

THE COUNTRY HOUSE IS MUCH IMPROVED WITH MODERN COMFORTS

THE ADVENT OF ELECTRICITY AND THE TELEPHONE ADDED GREATLY TO THE EASE OF RUNNING A COUNTRY HOUSE.

In its early days electricity was considered somewhat nouveau riche, if not downright vulgar, but this did not deter Sir William Armstrong. His Cragside in Northumberland was one of first British houses lit by electric light. Here in 1878, aided by the work of the Sunderland-born inventor Joseph Swan, inventor of the first practical light bulb, Armstrong installed a small hydroelectric plant on his estate for generating electric light in his picture gallery.

In 1880, electricity first became publicly supplied in Britain, but remained extremely expensive until the early

KEEPING IN TOUCH

For the master of a country house with business in London or other cities, the arrival of the telephone proved a boon. As with electricity, Hatfield House was a pioneer of this new technology. In the Duke of Portland's home at Welbeck Avenue he even employed, at the turn of the 20th century, his own telegrapher plus six engineers to care for his own electric plant. On a domestic level *Our Homes and How to Make them Healthy* commended the telephone for communication 'between a gentleman's residence and his stables or entrance lodge'.

20th century, making gas the popular choice for most country households. However the wider availability of electricity coincided with the arrival of the Arts and Crafts influence and, from the Edwardian period there was a steady proliferation of new 'electroliers' replacing gas fittings or gasoliers.

QUITE A SIGHT

In 1881, Hatfield House in Hertfordshire had electricity installed, both in the house itself and across the estate. Arriving there after sunset one day in 1890 the author Augustus Hare described the sight: *'All the windows blazed and glittered with light through the dark walls; the Golden Gallery with its hundreds of electric lamps was like a Venetian illumination.'*

IN EVERY HOUSE SOME APARTMENT SHOULD BE REGARDED AS THE SICK ROOM

WHEN ILLNESS STRUCK, PATIENTS WOULD BE TREATED BY A SICK NURSE. BECAUSE SO MANY INFECTIONS WERE FATAL, SICK ROOM HYGIENE WAS ALL-IMPORTANT.

Copious instructions were available for the positioning and running of the sick room. It needed to be dusted daily and all utensils removed and thoroughly cleansed or disinfected, especially in cases of contagion. Ideally, the room would catch the morning sun, it being 'easier to exclude the sun's rays than to dispense with them'. The bed needed to be placed out of a draught but away from the wall, and all valances and other hangings removed to improve ventilation. Flowers were permitted, particularly after Florence Nightingale declared them to be beneficial because they 'actually absorb carbonic acid and give off oxygen'.

The best employers took good care of the medical needs of the entire household, some even providing inoculations for staff and a salary and a house in the grounds for a doctor to attend to both family and staff.

ENSURING PERFECT CLEANLINESS

'Under all circumstances' said Mrs Beeton, 'the sick-room should be kept as fresh and sweet as the open air, while the temperature is kept up by artificial heat, taking care that the fire burns clear and gives out no smoke into the room; that the room is perfectly clean, wiped over with a damp cloth every day, if boarded; and swept, after sprinkling with damp tea-leaves, or other aromatic leaves, if carpeted; that all utensils are emptied and cleaned as soon as used, and not once in twenty-four hours as sometimes done.'

THE IDEAL NURSE

In cases of serious or long-term illness country house families employed qualified chamber nurses. *The Complete Servant* included the following guidelines for assessing her virtues and behaviour. She might also have to prepare medicines, weighing 'ingredients' with great accuracy using apothecaries' scales and liquid measures.

• Good temper, patience, watchfulness and sobriety are the cardinal virtues of a good nurse, and when possessed by one who unites skill with those personal qualities, she is a treasure above all price.

• She ought to be past the middle age, and if a married woman or widow, so much the better.

• She ought to be clean in her person, and neat in her dress, and free from habits of drinking or snuff-taking.

• She ought also to be a woman of cheerful and equable temper, and above all things, free from superstition, or belief in charms, omens, signs, dreams, and other follies of gross ignorance.

• Quietness in every respect, is of the first consequence…. Talking loud and whispering, so as to excite the suspicion of the patient, should be equally avoided.

• The nurse should scrupulously obey the instructions of the medical advisers, not only as the most likely means of promoting the speedy recovery of the patient, but to remove from herself all responsibility and blame.

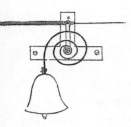

BELLS ARE AN ESSENTIAL MEANS OF COMMUNICATION

THEY MOST CERTAINLY WERE FROM THE 1760s, WHEN THE BELL PULL WAS INVENTED. PROPERLY WIRED, ARRAYS OF BELLS ALLOWED CONTACT WITH SERVANTS FROM ANY ROOM.

The standard set up of bells was to have pull cords or push buttons in the upstairs rooms and a row of bells in the basement or the servant's wing, each numbered to indicate the room where it had been rung. As systems became more sophisticated, with wires and cranks, it became possible to connect all the main living rooms, as well as the bedrooms, to the indicator board.

At Manderston in Berwickshire the bell-lever to the right of the fireplace in the morning room rang one of the 56 bells, each with a subtly different tone, ranked outside the housekeeper's room. The system is still in good working order. In smaller houses, speaking tubes were installed, using iron or gutta percha pipes into which messages could be shouted – and of course could be heard by all.

A WORKING SYSTEM

Advising on the installation of bells *Cassell's Household Guide* says that: 'Where a number of bells from different parts of the establishment are all brought together, they should be arranged on a bell board in a regular and systematic order – that is, the smallest and highest tones, should be at one end, and gradually range up to the deepest tones.'

CONVENIENT IMPROVEMENTS

With the arrival of electricity, modifications of the bell system became possible. As *Our Homes and How to Keep Them Healthy* of 1883 says, *'… electric and pneumatic bells are free from the inconvenience so common with ordinary bells – namely the stretching of the wires to such an extent as to involve difficulty in moving the bell sufficiently to make it sound.'* As to reliability it comments: *'The mechanism of the electric and pneumatic bell, especially the former, is far more simple than that of the ordinary bell, with its innumerable wires, cranks, levers, &c., all of which are easily put out of order.'*

COUNTRY HOUSE GUESTS SHOULD NEVER BE EXPECTED TO SHARE A ROOM

A DICTUM DATING TO THE 18TH CENTURY AND THE RISE OF THE COUNTRY HOUSE PARTY. THE EXCEPTIONS WERE BACHELORS WHO MIGHT BE ACCOMMODATED IN DORMITORIES KNOWN AS 'BARRACKS'.

In the early days of the country house, a bedroom or bedchamber was one of a suite of rooms, usually at ground floor level, and far from private. Here the occupant would not only sleep, but dine and receive visitors. Privacy was provided behind the curtains of the four-poster bed which by Tudor times was, in the wealthy country house, an enormous structure, with massive, richly carved pillars, embroidered and embellished curtains and the family coat of arms displayed at the head.

For family and guests

As country house residents gradually spent more time in communal rooms, so bedrooms, including the main or 'best' bedroom, moved upstairs. They still had dressing rooms attached, but were no longer public. For guests, bedrooms for married couples and single women were reasonably comfortable, and furnished with a couple of chairs and a writing table.

For bachelors, accommodation was much sparser and might be separated off into a wing of the house or placed on the top floor of the house – expressly to reduce their accessibility to women residents. At Kingston Lacy in Dorset, bachelors occupied 'tent rooms' on the attic floor, their sloping walls draped with striped awnings.

PERSONAL HYGIENE

Even in Victorian times, and often beyond, a bedroom would be supplied with a washstand containing a basin, jug and dishes for soap and a sponge. Ideally, advised *Our Homes and How to Make Them Healthy*, these *'... should be of the simplest possible construction, fitted up with tiles to a height of eighteen inches or two feet at the back, with as little woodwork as possible to get wet and dirty ... the centre might be fitted with a zinc receiver to take off the waste water ...'*

THE LIBRARY SHOULD BE A MOST HABITABLE ROOM

FROM THE MID 17TH CENTURY, THE COUNTRY HOUSE LIBRARY BECAME A PLACE FOR RELAXATION AS WELL AS READING. WITH BOOKS OFTEN STAMPED WITH THE FAMILY CREST IT WAS ALSO A STATUS SYMBOL.

The earliest country house libraries, like that of Sir William More at Losely in Surrey – which in 1556 contained 273 books – were private rooms adjoining the bedchamber. The books, being valuable possessions, were not openly displayed but kept in closets to protect them from both damp and smoke from open fires.

As family book collections grew, libraries became communal rooms for family and guests, although they were initially relatively small, and as well as serious tomes soon included lighter reading such as novels and plays. In the evenings the library might be used as a family sitting room, as Lady Grey of Wrest in Bedfordshire described in 1745: 'You can't imagine anything more cheerful than that room, nor more comfortable than reading there the rest of the evening.'

A COMFORTABLE PLACE

The need for comfort in a library is underlined by a Ham House inventory of 1679 which included '2 sleeping chayres, carv'd and guilt frames, covered with gould stuff with gould fringe'. Still in the house today there are wing armchairs with backs that can be adjusted with ratchets. By the late 18th century the library had become a place of entertainment, complete with games and scientific toys. Billiard tables were also installed.

A PLACE OF LEARNING

The library had a serious purpose, particularly in the Victorian era when the value of education was becoming more appreciated. Advising the aspiring country house owner *Our Homes and How to Make Them Healthy* says: '*The principle purpose for which a library is needed being the storage and study of books ... it must be dry and well lighted, but not exposed to direct sunlight... Plenty of wall-space must be provided for bookcases, and the bookcases should be all arranged for, and form part of the permanent architecture of the room. The windows, if deeply recessed, and of sufficient width, form convenient places for reading or writing, and, when so arranged, should each have a broad seat.*'

CARE OF FURNITURE IS THE RESPONSIBILITY OF THE GROOM OF THE CHAMBERS

JUST ONE OF THE MANY RESPONSIBILITIES OF THIS SERVANT TO WHOM THE UNDER BUTLER AND FOOTMEN WOULD REPORT.

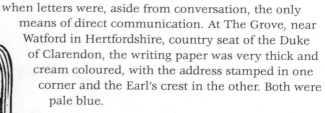

Every morning, the groom of the chambers was expected to brush down the furniture. Three or four times a day he needed to check in the reception rooms that the silver had been polished and that quills, pens and ink were well supplied on writing tables – essential items in an era when letters were, aside from conversation, the only means of direct communication. At The Grove, near Watford in Hertfordshire, country seat of the Duke of Clarendon, the writing paper was very thick and cream coloured, with the address stamped in one corner and the Earl's crest in the other. Both were pale blue.

A decreasing role

In a big house the groom of the chambers was expected to be trained in upholstery and to be able to hang wallpaper. In time, the role of groom of the chambers disappeared with many of his duties, such as closing the house up at night, being taken over by the head butler and his staff.

The groom of the chambers rang the bell for prayers and, if a house had a chapel, was responsible for setting out and removing kneelers before and after family prayers and for keeping the entire chapel clean. He would also:
- Brush the billiard table.
- Stand outside the door of the drawing room or library, to open it for guests as they came down for dinner.
- Assist in serving tea and coffee in the drawing room after dinner.
- Show arriving guests to their rooms.

PORTRAITS CAN BOTH COMMEMORATE AND ENTERTAIN

COLLECTING AND DISPLAYING PORTRAITS IN THE COUNTRY HOUSE – OF BOTH THE FAMILY AND OTHER NOTABLE FIGURES – BEGAN IN EARNEST IN THE 16TH CENTURY.

In Elizabethan times portraits, often bearing the family crest, were hung in the gallery to display the family's significance and mark their wealth. As galleries developed, so full-length portraits began to be painted to embellish them, as at Penshurst Place in Kent, where the Sidney family portraits remain on display. As well as portraits,

INSPIRATIONAL REMINDERS

Portraits were also intended to remind viewers of the great deeds of those depicted and to act as an inspiration. Remarking on a visit to Swakley's in Middlesex in 1665 Samuel Pepys recorded in his Diary: *'Pretty to see over the skreene of the hall ... the King's head, and my Lord of Essex on one side, and Fairfax on the other; upon the other side of the Skreene, the parson of the parish, and the lord of the manor and his sisters.'*

Like other household objects, portraits in oils needed to be well cared for.
• **Damp** – particularly injurious, rotting both canvases and wooden frames.
• **Direct sunlight** – faded the colours and made paint blister and crack.
• **Dust** – made pictures look dirty and needed to be removed. *Cassell's Household Guide* warned specifically against using soap, which was 'liable to assimilate with the paint on the picture and to make a lather of the colour itself'.

country house galleries contained busts of political figures whom the occupants admired, such as Charles James Fox, William Pitt the Younger, Martin Luther and Thomas Cranmer.

STAIRS TO SERVANTS' QUARTERS SHOULD NEVER BE OBVIOUS

AN ARCHITECTURAL DICTUM FROM THE VICTORIAN ERA,
AND A SHARP CONTRAST TO THE GRAND STAIRCASES
THAT WERE SYMBOLS OF WEALTH AND ELEGANCE.

Invisible servants' staircases were a consequence of the 'zoning' of houses, allowing staff access to different floors without being seen by the family or their guests. As the designer W.R. Lethaby (1857 – 1931) said 'it was the affectation of the time that work was done by magic; it was vulgar to recognize its existence or even to see anybody doing it.'

The very earliest Norman country houses had simple, narrow stone staircases spiralling to the upper floors. The grand staircase built around an open well was an innovation of the Elizabethan age, as at Burghley in Lincolnshire where, in imitation of the French style of the time, the wide steps, connected by landings, extended not only to the grand chamber on the first floor but right up to the roof. The trend continued in the Jacobean period, when staircases became ornately decorated, as at Hatfield House in Hertfordshire.

In superior style

Classic elegance was the hallmark of the Georgian staircase, which was made using cantilever technology and decorated with delicate carvings. More glamorous yet were the Regency staircases in which a single central staircase branched into two, one branch leading to each side of the upper floor, as at Heaton Hall in Lancashire, designed by James Wyatt. The staircase was the perfect place for pageantry, notably at the height of the country house seasons of the 19th and early 20th centuries, when guests might well desire to 'make an entrance'.

NURSERY FURNITURE SHOULD BE AS PLAIN AS POSSIBLE, EASILY CLEANED AND MOVABLE

A SAYING REFLECTING THE CLOSE ATTENTION TO HEALTH NECESSARY IN AN ERA WHEN CHILD DEATHS WERE COMMONPLACE.

In a large house, the children's nursery consisted typically of two or more upstairs rooms conveniently close to those of the servants, although this arrangement meant that a great deal of time and energy was spent carrying items up and down stairs. However it was deemed unsanitary for sinks to be situated on the same floor as the nursery, chiefly to avoid the temptation of emptying chamber pots into them. Or as *Our Homes and How to Make Them Healthy* said: 'The manifest

FOR THE CHILDREN

The ideal nursery bedroom was spacious and airy with a high ceiling. It was never used during the daytime except for naps. And, as *The Complete Servant* prescribed: '*No servants should sleep in the same room, nor ought any thing to be done there that may contaminate the air, in which so great a portion of infantine life is to be spent. The consequences of vitiated [defective] air in bed-rooms*', it warned, are '*often fatal. Feather-bed and bed curtains ought to be proscribed, as tending to debility; neither ought the beds to be placed too low, as the most pernicious stratum of air is that nearest the floor.*'

convenience of having a sink near to rid the nursery department of soiled water has to be weighed against the tendency of all servants to misuse such convenience, and it is best to decide against such sources of mischief.'

SIMPLE AND SAFE

Nursery furniture was plain and undecorated, consisting of cupboards and wooden high chairs and cots that could be easily cleaned, and the open fire protected with a fender of wire mesh topped with a brass rail. Windows were fenced with bars, or the lower sashes nailed down to prevent them from being opened.

The simple 'citizen's furniture' designed by Philip Webb and made by the company founded by William Morris in 1861 was regarded as highly suitable for a Victorian nursery. Also popular was the bentwood furniture such as the rocking chairs introduced in the 1830s by Messrs Thonet of Vienna.

AN ENTIRE SUITE OF ROOMS MAY BE SET ASIDE FOR ROYALTY

A COMMON CUSTOM IN LARGE HOUSES FREQUENTED BY
ROYAL VISITORS. ACCOMMODATION WITH SUFFICIENT
PRIVACY ALSO NEEDED TO BE SECURED FOR THEIR STAFF.

Royal suites in country houses might be exquisitely
furnished. Among the items in the state bedroom at
Lowther Castle in Cumbria in the early 20th century were
embroidered silk Japanese hangings, furniture originally
from Versailles and a carpet originally woven on the
Lowther estate. In more modest houses without royal
suites, a huge amount of work was needed ahead of a royal
visit to ensure that everything was in perfect order, which
might involve the complete redecoration of rooms and
reupholstering of furniture. If there was direct access to the
garden, then this would be kept exclusively for royal use
during the visit.

Staff arrangements

It was necessary for private secretaries and the like to be
able to come and go easily, not least because the post and
telegraph would still bring daily duties for the monarch,
such as reading state papers. Arrangements for royal staff,
made by the steward or housekeeper, needed to provide
privacy and comply with staff etiquette. Royal staff would
take their meals in specific rooms and needed to know their
appointed place in the hierarchy of the table according to
seniority and length of service.

ESSENTIALS OF ETIQUETTE

Detailing the requirements for *'entertaining their Majesties'* Mary Spencer Warren, writing in *The Lady's Realm* of 1904, specified that separate suites should be provided for the King, the Queen, and any other members of the Royal Family and consist of *'a sleeping apartment, a dressing-room, a bath-room, breakfast-room, study or writing-room and a drawing or reception-room'*. These should be *'furnished in accordance with the well-known tastes of these distinguished personages'* and be *'quite remote from those occupied by other guests in order that perfect quiet and retirement may be secured, as well as facilities for the transaction of government and other state business.'*

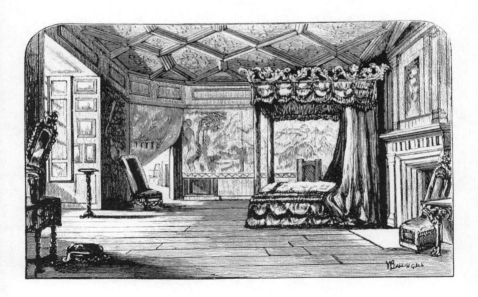

THE
DAILY
ROUTINE

From early morning until late at night country house servants were tirelessly engaged in the myriad tasks needed to keep the home clean, tidy and running smoothly. The precise timetable for each day – and day of the week – varied remarkably little from house to house, but the details of the routine varied for each member of the household staff.

Individual routines

While maids were busiest in the mornings, preparing for the business of the day, the services of footmen were required from before breakfast and throughout the afternoon and evening. For valets and ladies' maids the day could not end until the master and mistress of the house had retired to bed, while the butler needed to make sure that the house was properly secured before he could finally get some rest. Laundry was seen to on several days of each week, beginning on a Monday. Time was set aside, particularly during the summer months, for activities such as making preserves and salting meat to ensure supplies throughout the year. During the shooting and hunting seasons, and at Christmas and times of family celebration, there were many special meals to prepare.

The demands of the bell

Whatever the time of day, the sound of a bell demanded immediate attention from servants. For the family, the day also ran to a strict routine, with set times for meals, prayers and leisure activities. Calling, whether as host or guests was almost always an afternoon pursuit. When there were children in the house their day was rigidly organized by the governess with set times for meals, lessons, play and seeing their parents.

SCULLERY MAIDS MUST BE THE EARLIEST RISERS

INEVITABLY, IT WAS THE DUTY OF THESE LOWLIEST SERVANTS TO GET THE COUNTRY HOUSE READY FOR THE DAY, BEGINNING AT ABOUT 5.30 AM.

Once she had risen from her small, sparsely furnished quarters under the eaves, the first task for the scullery maid – who might have been only 13 or 14 years old – was to scrub and sweep the kitchen areas and clear the ashes from the fire grate if this had not been done the night before. She then wiped over the kitchen range, which also needed to be blackleaded every two or three days to keep it clean and rust free. The range fire was then re-laid and lit, and fires lit under any of the coppers or boilers needed for heating water.

Many duties

Next, the scullery maid had to distribute hot water for the senior servants and lay breakfast in the servants' hall. She then began washing up plates

---

ESSENTIAL RECIPE

Blackleading for the range had to be made ahead of time. The Victorian manual *Enquire Within* included this popular recipe for a messy job:

'[Take] half a pound of black lead finely powdered, and (to make it stick) mix it with the white of three eggs well beaten; then dilute it with sour beer or porter till it becomes as thin as shoe-blacking; after stirring it, set it over hot coals to simmer for twenty minutes; when cold it may be kept for use.'

and dishes and, as detailed in *The Complete Servant* of 1675, needed to take care that all utensils were 'always kept clean, dry and fit for use.' She was also expected 'to assist the kitchen maid in picking, trimming, washing and boiling the vegetables, cleaning the kitchen and offices, the servants' hall, housekeeper's room, and steward's room, and to clean the steps of the front door and area.'

THE BEST ADVICE

Although acknowledging that the role of scullery maid *'is not, of course, one of high rank'* Mrs Beeton insisted that *'if she be fortunate enough to have over her a good kitchen-maid and clever cook, she may very soon learn to perform various little duties connected with cooking operations, which may be of considerable service in fitting her for a more responsible place.'*

FOOTMEN ARE EXPECTED TO RISE BEFORE THE FAMILY ARE STIRRING

AN EARLY START WAS NECESSARY FOR GETTING THE DIRTIEST JOBS COMPLETED BEFORE FOOTMEN WERE CALLED ON TO PERFORM THEIR MANY OTHER DUTIES.

Once boots and shoes had been attended to, footmen needed to see to the furniture using an oil, or some other preparation of the right colour, to treat the wood of everything from tables and chairs to sideboards. Once applied, oil had to be rubbed off quickly, then each item polished with a clean cloth. Wax was best put on sparingly, then rubbed off with a separate cloth. While doing his morning cleaning the footman needed a white apron to hand; he would have to don this quickly should he be called

THE MIRROR EFFECT

Being expensive, mirrors needed particular care. The frames would never be allowed to get wet or damp. Early 19th-century instructions ran: *'First, take a clean, soft sponge, just squeezed out of water, and then dipped in spirits of wine; rub the glass over with this, and then polish it off with fine powder blue, or whiting tied up in muslin, quickly laid on, and then well rubbed off, with a clean cloth, and afterwards with a silk handkerchief.'*

CLEANER BOOTS AND SHOES

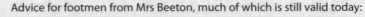

Advice for footmen from Mrs Beeton, much of which is still valid today:
• Three good brushes and good blacking must be provided; one of the brushes hard, to brush off the mud; the other soft, to lay on the blacking; the third of a medium hardness, for polishing.
• The blacking should be kept corked up … and applied to the brush with a sponge tied to a stick which, when put away, rests in a notch in the cork.
• When boots come in very muddy … wash off the mud, and wipe them dry with a sponge; then leave them to dry very gradually on their sides, taking care they are not placed near the fire, or scorched.
• Much delicacy of treatment is required in cleaning ladies' boots, so as to make the leather look well-polished, and the upper part retain a fresh appearance, with the lining free from hand marks, which are very offensive to a lady of refined tastes.
• Patent leather boots require to be wiped with a wet sponge, and afterwards with a soft, dry cloth…. A little milk may be used with very good effect for patent leather boots.

away to answer the door or wait at the breakfast table.

The Complete Servant, expanding on the early morning duties of the footman, lists his jobs as: 'cleaning the shoes and boots, knives and forks, brushing and cleaning clothes, hats and gloves and cleaning the furniture, &c. &c.' He might also clean lamps and pump and carry water. To save his livery from being dirtied he was advised to wear 'a pair of overalls, a waistcoat and fustian [heavy cotton] jacket, and a leather apron'.

FAMILY PRAYERS ARE SAID A QUARTER OF AN HOUR BEFORE BREAKFAST

THIS DAILY GATHERING, ANNOUNCED BY A GONG RUNG BY THE FOOTMAN, WAS ATTENDED BY ALL HOUSEHOLD MEMBERS. EVERYONE WOULD ALSO ATTEND CHURCH ON SUNDAYS.

Prayers were traditionally held in the country house chapel, if there was one, or in the library, hall or dining room, and included children brought down from the nursery. Usually held at 8.30 and lasting some 15 minutes, they were led by the master of the house or, if he was not in residence, by the mistress, with everyone kneeling or standing with heads bowed.

Before putting on clean aprons, straightening their caps and going upstairs for prayers, kitchen staff (who would have already eaten) would make sure that everything was ready for serving breakfast immediately afterwards, with cooked dishes kept warm. Following prayers family

GOD-GIVEN DUTIES

The link between service and godliness was avidly encouraged with the display of religious texts in the servants' quarters, the giving of Bibles as gifts, and even in hymns. The English churchman John Keble (1792 – 1866) penned these telling lines:

The trivial round, the
*   common task,*
Will furnish all we need to
*   ask,*
Room to deny ourselves, a
*   road*
To bring us daily nearer God.

While a century earlier the Welsh poet George Herbert (1593 – 1633) proffered these instructions:

Teach me, my God and King,
In all things Thee to see,
And what I do in anything,
To do it as for Thee.

A servant with this clause
Makes drudgery divine;
Who sweeps a room as for
*   Thy laws,*
Makes that and the action fine.

announcements – and possibly open reprimands for staff – were made before the servants filed out.

Sunday best

For Sunday morning services, whether in the chapel or at a nearby church reached on foot, servants always dressed soberly. As an Edwardian servant Doris Bodger recalls: '… we had to wear black coats and skirts, black shoes, stockings and gloves, and a hat which was called a toque which made a young girl of thirteen look like a grandmother.' While the family sat in reserved front pews, servants occupied the back pews or the gallery, seated according to their rank. On alternate Sundays servants might also be expected to attend afternoon or evening services, which greatly reduced their leisure time.

THE BEDROOMS ARE CLEANED AFTER BREAKFAST

A DAILY DUTY FOR HOUSEMAIDS, WHICH ALSO INCLUDED ATTENDING TO DRESSING ROOMS. LADIES' MAIDS WOULD PERFORM SIMILAR DUTIES FOR THEIR MISTRESSES.

Seeing to the bedrooms began with opening the windows to let the room air (or the door only in cold weather) and, if necessary, emptying chamber pots. The bed covers were then stripped off and hung over chair backs to air while the mattress was shaken. Next the housemaid might clean out the fireplace and re-lay the fire before going downstairs to wash her hands and put on a clean apron. On her return she would make each bed before brushing the carpet, dusting

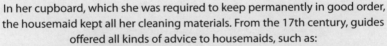

FROM THE HOUSEMAID'S CUPBOARD

In her cupboard, which she was required to keep permanently in good order, the housemaid kept all her cleaning materials. From the 17th century, guides offered all kinds of advice to housemaids, such as:

• **Dusting carpets and floors**: Carpets should not be swept with a whisk-brush more than once a week; at other times sprinkle damp tea-leaves on them, and sweep them carefully, then brush them gently with a clothes brush.

• **To clean marble**: Mix up the strongest soap-lees with quicklime until it has the consistency of milk, and leave it on the marble for 24 hours. Then clean it with soap and water.

• **To clean floorcloth** (a waxed canvas used in servants' quarters): Wash with a damp flannel, wet it all over with milk and rub it well with a dry cloth; a most beautiful polish will be brought out.

• **If drawers come out stiffly**: Rub over the spot where they press with a little soap.

A COMPLETE AIRING

To make sure that a bed was properly aired a housemaid might use this method recommended by *Enquire Within:* *'Introduce a drinking glass between the sheets for a minute or two, just when the warming-pan is taken out; if the bed be dry, there will only be a slight cloudy appearance on the glass, but if not, the damp of the bed will collect in and on the glass....'*

the furniture, dusting or washing any ornaments and making sure that carafes of fresh water were placed in each room.

After the cleaning had been done the housekeeper inspected each bedroom and dressing room, making sure that towels, soap, writing-paper, and inkstands had been attended to, and that all drawers and wardrobes had been properly dusted.

Additional duties

Junior housemaids were also required to see to the upper servants' beds and sweep and dust their rooms. Later in the day, while the family and guests were dining, she would take hot water to each bedroom and, especially in winter, add a warming pan to the bed to prepare it for the night.

DAILY STORES ARE APPORTIONED BY THE HOUSEKEEPER

AS GUARDIAN OF THE STOREROOM KEY, THE
HOUSEKEEPER WAS IN CHARGE OF ALL PROVISIONS,
INCLUDING FLOUR, RICE, SUGAR, TEA AND COFFEE.

Stores for each day were given out by the housekeeper once all the arrangements for family breakfast were in order, after which she would check the stillroom. Throughout the day she supervised the various maids. In the late afternoon, following tea, she was responsible for pounding and grinding spices, washing and picking over currants, stoning raisins and breaking up the large loaves in which sugar was supplied, then pounding and rolling it into fine grains. She might also pare oranges and lemons and set aside the rinds to dry; they would later be grated and added to a variety of dishes.

ODE TO A HOUSEKEEPER

The perfect housekeeper was lauded in verse in the 1850s by Philip Yorke II of Erdigg in North Wales. A competent cook might well be promoted to this role.

Upon the portly frame we look
Of one who was our former Cook.
No better keeper of our Store,
Did ever enter at our door.
She knew and pandered to our taste,
Allowed no want and yet no waste.

"Excellent, Most delicate, and Refreshing." "The Queen."

CHOICE IN LEADS PACKETS DULCEMONA TEA

YOUNG, FRESH, INVIGORATING

1/6 to 3/- Per lb of all first class Grocers.

THE ONLY TEA SELECTED FOR THE EMPIRE OF INDIA EXHIBITION, 1895.

AND FANCY TINS.

Of good character

Like the butler, the housekeeper needed to be a person of integrity and experience who had either kept house herself or had a long record of service. A mature woman, both in age and demeanour was deemed essential and she was always addressed as 'Mrs', whether or not she was married. As well as provisions, the housekeeper was responsible for all the linen of the house, for which she would keep an inventory.

WINE FOR THE DAY SHOULD BE DECANTED IN THE MORNING

JUST ONE OF MANY DUTIES OF THE BUTLER, THE MAN RESPONSIBLE FOR EVERYTHING TO DO WITH ALCOHOLIC BEVERAGES.

The country house cellar was the butler's domain, and his cellar book the record of every bottle held within it (including sherry and port as well as wine and champagne) and its date of entry and exit. Wine purchase, however, was the responsibility of the master of the house, who was, unless he trusted his butler implicitly, keeper of the key to the wine cellar. Decanting was essential to separate off deposits or dregs accumulated within bottles.

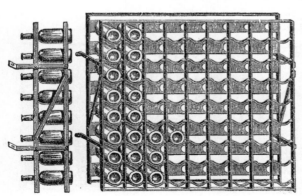

When decanting, the butler was advised to use a wine strainer lined with a fine material such as cambric. The art lay in pouring the wine into the decanter slowly and steadily.

To clarify and stabilize it, wine was 'fined' by the butler then bottled by him, often as early as 4 or 5 in the morning. These instructions are based on those recommended by Mrs Beeton:

Fining

1. Take a gallon of wine and whisk a quart of it with the whites of four eggs.
2. Pour back into the cask through the bunghole.
3. Stir up the whole cask, using a clean split stick moved in a 'rotatory direction'.
4. Pour in the remainder of the wine drawn off.
5. Stir again, skimming off any bubbles that rise to the surface.
6. Close the bunghole and leave to stand for three or four days.

Bottling – best done with two people, one to draw off the wine, the other to cork the bottles.

1. Thoroughly wash and dry the bottles.
2. Soak corks in hot water.
3. Bore a hold in the lower part of the cask with a gimlet, 'receiving the liquid stream which follows in the bottle and filterer, which is placed in a tub or basin' to avoid waste. As the bottom of the cask is reached, put a thick piece of muslin over the filter to prevent 'viscous grounds' from entering the bottle.
4. Make sure each bottle is filled 'up to the mark' but not too full.
5. Drive in the corks with a wooden mallet.
6. Count, record and store the bottles.

Because of his position, the butler needed to be a man of integrity, but insobriety was a common failing of butlers, for which dismissal was inevitable if discovered. He also needed to be sure that drinks never fell into the wrong hands.

KNIVES AND OTHER CUTLERY ARE ATTENDED TO IN THE BUTLER'S PANTRY

CLEANING AND SHARPENING KNIVES WAS A MORNING TASK FOR THE HALLBOY OR A FOOTMAN. KNIFE CLEANING MIGHT ALSO BE A JOB FOR THE UNDER GARDENER.

Seeing to cutlery was a lengthy business in any large country house. Knives, which stained and rusted easily before the advent of stainless steel, needed particular attention. First they needed to be carefully washed in hot water with a little salt added to remove every trace of grease, but without immersing their handles which, if made of ivory, could become discoloured and loose if placed in hot water.

Next, knife blades were dried, then rubbed on a knife board covered with brick dust or, as gadgets advanced, inserted into a rotary knife

HELP FROM GADGETS

Machines to assist with cleaning knives and other cutlery were as great a boon as this 1850s advertisement from the *The Illustrated Times* suggests:
KNIVES CLEANED by the old brick-dust board are rapidly worn out, by some machines they are notched or blunted, but others no time or labour is saved, while all are very expensive; but by the Patent Press Knife and Fork Cleaner, which cannot get out of order, all these evils are avoided, at a price to suit the most economical. Prices: To clean six knives, &c., 14s; 12 ditto, 20s; 18 dittos, 25s; 24 dittos, 30s. Oliver Long, patentee and manufacturer.

cleaning machine into which a patent powder had been shaken (See Help from gadgets). Care was essential. If pushed in too far the knife shoulders would get worn and their edges blunted. Any knives not needed immediately were rubbed with mutton suet to exclude air and help prevent them from rusting.

Precious metal

Silver cutlery was the footmen's responsibility. It was washed in hot water every day and wiped, then buffed up with a soft rag or leather. Weekly – or more often, depending on how much it was used – it was cleaned with a paste made from whiting mixed with ammonia and cold water or with rags boiled in a mixture of hartshorn powder (ammonium carbonate) and water.

> ### Many tasks
> The hallboy was the most junior of male staff, often a local boy who still lived at home with his parents. As well as cleaning knives he might see to lamps, clean boots and shoes (if these were not done by a junior footman) and even groom dogs.

ATTENTION TO LAUNDRY BEGINS ON A MONDAY MORNING

IT IS NO MYTH THAT BEFORE THE ADVENT OF THE WASHING MACHINE LAUNDRY TOOK MOST OF THE WEEK TO COMPLETE, STARTING ON MONDAY.

The biggest country houses had detached laundries consisting of a series of rooms including a wash house or washing room, drying room and hot air closet, mangling room and an ironing and folding room. A team of laundry maids began by collecting and sorting everything by fabric – white linen and collars; sheets and body linen; fine muslins; coloured cotton and linen; woollens; and coarse kitchen and greasy cloths. Keeping track of the laundry was ultimately the housekeeper's responsibility, but every laundry maid had to keep exact lists of every item in the 'washing book'.

A long soak

Soaking was the next task, for all but the woollens and the finest items, and done either in washing troughs or in buckets fitted with draining devices at the base. Each piece was folded then immersed in lukewarm water (ideally rainwater, which was often collected for the purpose) with lye added. Except for the dirtiest clothes they could then simply be rinsed and dried before being starched, if necessary, and ironed.

The scale of the wash

A Victorian inventory of linen for Shugborough in Staffordshire gives an idea of the scale of laundry tasks and included:
85 dozen damask tablecloths and the same number of napkins
67 diaper (patterned linen) tablecloths
60 pairs each of sheets and pillowcases of a variety of quality
37 towels

TUESDAY AND WEDNESDAY ARE THE DAYS FOR WASHING AND DRYING

AFTER MONDAY CAME MORE ARDUOUS TASKS FOR THE LAUNDRY MAIDS.

Firing up the copper boilers was the prelude to washing heavily soiled items, which were immersed and rubbed clean, often with hard yellow soap. Soda might be added. Laundry maids suffered greatly from constantly immersing their hands and arms in the hot water, but were helped by washboards and dollies (long handled wooden objects with four or five legs that looked rather like upside down milking stools). The laundry was then rinsed in cold water and, to remove excess water, items were either twisted – often with

ADVICE FOR LAUNDRY MAIDS

Cassell's Household Guide **advises that:** *'Sheets and table-cloths should be hung with the short side towards the wind, to enable the air to blow the folds apart. Shirts should be suspended from the bottom hem.'* **Anything unsuitable for hanging on a line with wooden pegs was put onto racks or clotheshorses in the drying room.**

one end attached to a hook on the wall – or, even better,
passed through the rollers of a hand-cranked wringer.

Getting it dry

For drying, hanging laundry such as sheets and tablecloths
outside where sunlight could bleach out any stains was
ideal. In inclement weather, all the laundry had to be dried
indoors. From the mid 19th century, country houses had
drying closets – brick enclosures built over the hot water
pipes or the furnaces used for heating the house. Inside
were long iron frames that slid in and out. The air needed to
circulate freely within the closets to prevent laundry from
yellowing.

MANGLING, STARCHING AND IRONING ARE CARRIED OUT AT THE END OF THE WEEK

THESE WERE THE LAST STAGES OF THE LAUNDRY
PROCESS, USUALLY DONE ON THURSDAYS AND FRIDAYS
WELL AWAY FROM THE WASH HOUSE.

The mangle, although now associated with removing
water from clothes, was an invention originally used
for flattening washed and dried sheets and tablecloths,

and any simple clothes without frills. In the box mangle, clothes were wrapped around wooden cylinders and rolled to and fro by turning a wheel, with pressure applied from above. Alternatively they could be fed through the rollers of an upright mangle. After mangling, linens would be flattened further in a linen press.

The essential stiffener

Starch was vital for stiffening everything from linen tablecloths to shirtfronts and collars before they were mangled, pressed or ironed. Glenfield Patent Starch, used in the Royal Laundry of Queen Victoria was widely advertised as available from 'all Chandlers, Grocers, &c., &c.', but households would make their own starch. For shirtfronts, a cold starch made by melting wax in water was used, while for larger items a paste of ready-bought starch and hot water was preferred. For economy, starch could be made from ground rice, wheat or potato flour.

ALL ABOUT IRONS

Any necessary pressing and ironing was carried out with flat irons heated on a stove or with box irons equipped with hollow containers filled with slugs of metal, heated on the fire. Alternatively a receptacle at the back of the iron contained heated charcoal.

For ruffles and flounces a gauffering iron was essential. This gadget, shaped like a metal test tube, was set horizontally on a stand and heated by inserting a metal poker-like rod fresh from stove or hearth. Around it, frilled cuffs and collars could be curled. For rows of frilled trimmings, heated gauffering or crimping tongs were used.

YOUNG CHILDREN MUST BE TAKEN OUT FOR A WALK EACH MORNING AND AFTERNOON

PART OF THE UNBREAKABLE DAILY NURSERY ROUTINE WHICH, AS IN THE REST OF THE HOUSE, BEGAN IN THE EARLY HOURS.

The nursery maid, the most junior member of the nursery staff, was the first to rise, at about six in the morning, when she would light the fire and complete any cleaning before the children arose at around seven. At 7.30 children were bathed and dressed before breakfast, prepared by the nursery maid, was served. The nurse, to whom she reported, was a highly regarded staff member, usually well treated by their mistresses but often 'tyrannical and overbearing'.

A MATTER OF TIMING

'Sometimes' said *The Servants' Practical Guide* *'children are brought down after instead of before tea, five o'clock being the hour for nursery-tea; but as half-past five is near to the hour of young children's bed-time, they are rather inclined to be cross and sleepy if taken to the drawing-room after they have had their tea.'*

Daily exercise

A walk, taken at 9.30 in summer and 11.00 in winter, was the main morning activity but should not, advised *The Complete Servant*, be 'long enough to fatigue them'. If there were two or more children, the nursery maid would accompany the nurse. On their return, older children would attend to their lessons while younger ones lay down to rest.

Following their main meal – originally known as 'dinner' – and weather permitting, children were taken out again for an hour and a half in the afternoon, then washed and tidied

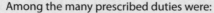

THE NURSERY MAID'S DUTIES

Among the many prescribed duties were:
- Sweep and dust the day nursery, clean the grate and light the fire.
- Bring up the bath water. Assist the nurse in washing and dressing the children.
- Lay the nursery breakfast and dinner tables, then clear away and wash up afterwards.
- Make the beds and empty the baths.
- Sweep and clean the night nursery.
- Amuse the children before tea.
- Help the nurse in preparing the children's things for wear the next morning.
- Mend children's clothes and make new garments.

up before being taken by the nurse to the drawing room at 4.30. There they would be left with their mother (and possibly their father) for about half an hour before returning to the nursery for tea.

A GOOD GOVERNESS ADHERES TO A STRICT TIMETABLE

AS IN THE NURSERY, THE STRICT SCHOOLROOM TIMETABLE WAS SET TO SYNCHRONIZE WITH THE ROUTINE IN THE REST OF THE HOUSE.

Even before breakfast, older children might be obliged to practise the piano or another musical instrument. With breaks for meals and walks, lessons could last for up to eight hours a day, continuing even after nursery tea and time spent with parents.

Since many governesses were woman who had fallen on hard times, some undoubtedly took out their disappointment and bitterness on the children in their care. Even the most well-meaning often found it hard to build a friendship and rapport with their pupils and discipline was paramount, with bad behaviour often severely punished with slapping and beating. Yet many governesses were much loved by their pupils.

A WOMAN OF MANY TALENTS

Expanding on the qualities of the perfect governess, *The Complete Servant* **said that:** *'In addition to a thorough knowledge of the English Language, and to the power of being able to write a letter in a graceful and accurate style, the governess ought to be moderately acquainted with the French Language; and it would be an advantage if she knew something of Italian, as the language of music. She ought also be able to play the pianoforte... It will be also expected that she shall be able to teach the elements of dancing, at least, the steps and ordinary figures of fashionable practice.'*

Academic studies

The governess was required to be knowledgeable in '…the useful art of arithmetic, the constant exercise of which will so much improve the reasoning power of her pupils' and there was no reason why she should 'omit to introduce to her pupils the geographical copy books, and other elementary books of geography, by Goldsmith; and the familiar keys to popular sciences'. Other subjects added to the list were drawing and needlework plus 'religion, morals and temper'.

IT IS CUSTOMARY FOR THE SERVANTS TO DINE WHILST THE FAMILY TAKE LUNCHEON

AN IMPORTANT BREAK FOR BUSY COUNTRY HOUSE SERVANTS TO GIVE THEM ENERGY FOR MANY HOURS OF WORK AHEAD.

This was originally the main meal of the day for staff, served in the servants' hall at 1 o'clock. When dinner moved to a later hour for master and mistress, the servants followed suit. Usually, both upper and lower servants dined together in the servants' hall, but if there was a house steward, he and the housekeeper might dine together in either of their rooms. Or senior staff might partake of selected dishes only.

Meat was a staple of servants' dinners. At Cannons, the Middlesex home of the Duke of Chandos, each 18th-century servant was served 21 oz (600 g) of beef on Tuesday,

WELL FED STAFF

'England knows nothing of separate cooking for servants, who partake of all the courses sampled by the masters, the latter having first choice and the servants what remains....' **So said the German novelist Sophie von la Roche commenting on staff meals on a visit to England in the late 18th century. However the lower servants might be denied proper rations by their superiors below stairs.**

Thursday and Sunday, the same amount of mutton on Monday and Friday; and 14 oz (400 g) of pork on Wednesday and Saturday. In addition they were given 'pastries, jellies, tarts, and all good things prized by the master'.

Ale and beer were habitually drunk, a pint being the usual serving. In some houses staff were offered 'beer money' in place of the beverage, which might be spent by men in the local hostelry.

ON HER VISITS, THE LADY OF THE HOUSE IS ACCOMPANIED BY A FOOTMAN

AFTERNOON WAS THE USUAL TIME FOR LADIES TO MAKE VISITS, BUT THE FOOTMAN, WHO ORIGINALLY WALKED OR RAN ALONGSIDE A COACH, MIGHT BE NEEDED AT ANY TIME.

In a house with three or more footmen, the 'lady's footman' was the second most senior and spared the dirtiest jobs. When accompanying his mistress in a carriage, a footman dressed in his best livery with clean shoes and well-brushed hat and greatcoat. He received instructions from his mistress as she entered the carriage – climbing the steps he had already put up for her – and delivered these to the coachman. When shutting the carriage door he needed to take extreme care not to 'injure any one, or the dresses of the ladies'.

The lady's footman was also responsible for carrying all her messages and delivering her invitations, and to accompany her should she wish to go out on foot. He might also prepare her breakfast and wait behind her chair at both breakfast and dinner. If she went out riding he would clasp his hands together so that she could step onto them to mount her horse.

FOR PERFECT COMFORT

A well-prepared lady's footman had umbrellas, rugs – and even a stone hot water bottle – always to hand to ensure his mistress's comfort whilst travelling. He also ensured that the interior of the carriage was spotlessly clean and free from dust.

AFTERNOON TEA IS SERVED IN THE DRAWING ROOM

TEA WAS NOT MERELY A FORM OF REFRESHMENT BUT AN OCCASION FOR LADIES, ESPECIALLY, TO EXCHANGE NEWS AND GOSSIP AND TO PLAN THEIR SOCIAL LIVES.

By the Victorian era, when luncheon was eaten and dinner served in the evening, tea was customarily taken in the afternoon. Mrs Beeton gives a vivid description of the scene at which both tea and coffee were served, poured by the hostess: 'As soon as the drawing-room bell rings for tea, the footman enters with the tray, which has been previously prepared; hands the tray round to the company, with cream and sugar, the tea and coffee being generally poured out, while another attendant hands out cakes, toast, or biscuits.'

'Grand' teas, with visitors, were timed for five o'clock. A few men might be present, but they were a rarity. Food was often served buffet-style with a choice of bread and butter, sandwiches, biscuits, ices and fruit; wine and claret cup would also be offered.

AFTER THE CHASE

Tea in the warmth of the house was also relished by sportsmen and women. As Agnes Jekyll says in her *Kitchen Essays* of 1922: *'Hungry hunters and shooters, triumphant from the chase, love to quench their thirst and spoil their dinners under the stuffed heads in the great hall.... The true spiritual home of the tea-pot is surely in a softly-lighted room, between a deep arm-chair and a sofa cushioned with Asiatic charm ....'

IT IS THE FOOTMAN'S DUTY TO LAY THE DINNER TABLE

AS WELL AS THESE TASKS, CLOSELY SUPERVISED BY THE BUTLER, HE WAS ALSO OBLIGED TO SERVE AT MEALS THROUGHOUT THE DAY.

Before the cutlery, glasses and ornaments were set out, the dinner table was covered with a thick baize cloth over which was placed a fine white damask tablecloth. The footman needed to make sure that this cloth, and the damask serviettes (napkins), had been properly ironed and aired in the laundry (see Attention to laundry begins on Monday morning). Small engraved carafes, or water bottles, were placed on each side of the table, one to each couple. One silver or fine glass salt cellar was similarly positioned.

Before dinner the footman needed to be properly dressed in his livery with white tie and spotless white cotton gloves. Whilst waiting during

THE FULL COVER

For a dinner party the usual cover for each person comprised, said *The Servants' Practical Guide: 'Two large dinner-knives and a small silver fish-knife; two large dinner-forks and a small silver fish-fork; these are placed on the right and left-hand side of the space to be occupied by the plate, a table-spoon for soup is also placed on the right-hand side, bowl upwards.'* **Dessert spoons and knives for fruit and cheese were handed only when these dishes were served.**

'A glass for sherry, a glass for hock or claret (whichever is given) and a glass for champagne' **placed at the right-hand side were also recommended. It adds that** *'A tumbler is not used at a dinner-party unless the guest does not drink wine, when a tumbler would be asked for of a servant in attendance.'*

MEASURED EXACTLY

When all was ready on the table the butler examined it closely, measuring each setting with a ruler to ensure that all were perfectly equal. He also placed any precious silver items on the table himself.

THE DUITES OF DINNER

The footman's role in dinner service ran like this:
- Ring the bell about half an hour before dinner.
- Carry up everything that is likely to be needed before and during the meal on trays.
- Prepare the drawing room, lighting the fire.
- Announce in the drawing room that dinner is served.
- Stand behind his master or mistress.
- Hand dishes around for all courses.
- Take away dish covers removed by the butler.

And following dinner …
- Clear the table.
- Put away the plate (silver).
- Wash the glass and silver.
- Prepare and assist in carrying tea and coffee to the drawing room.
- Attend to the requirements of the gentlemen in the smoking room.
- Be in attendance in the front hall when guests are leaving.
- Bring candles or lamps for the members of the household before they retire to bed.

dinner the footman was required to be 'obtrusive to none', to hand food to the left side of each diner and to hold dishes so that food could be taken with ease. 'In lifting dishes from the table' says Mrs Beeton, 'he should use both hands, and remove them with care'.

Extra duties

As well as serving at dinner the footman set and waited at the breakfast table, and cleared the room afterwards, sweeping up any crumbs, shaking out the baize cloth and replacing the tablecloth. At teatime he carried up the tray holding toast and muffins. He also answered the door, greeting and announcing guests.

A MASTER'S APPEARANCE IS THE RESPONSIBILITY OF HIS VALET

BOTH AT HOME AND AWAY, ATTENDING TO THE WARDROBE WAS A MAJOR ROLE FOR THE VALET WHO CARED FOR ALL HIS EMPLOYER'S PERSONAL NEEDS.

Early each morning, before his master arose, the valet needed to be sure that his dressing gown and slippers were airing before the fire and his clean linen perfectly ready. Clothes, brushed the previous night, were placed over the backs of chairs, right sides out and boots cleaned by him, not another servant. Clean water for washing would be ready, along with pristine hair, nail and toothbrushes. If a gentleman did not shave himself, then it was essential that the razor was first stropped on a leather to sharpen it, having first been warmed by being dipped in hot water. The valet then helped his master on with his clothes.

Discretion and polish were prime qualities in a valet. He also needed to:
- Have a short memory.
- Be cautious of mischief-making.
- Pack clothes for his master on visits away from the house, including special dress for outdoor activities and formal dinners.
- Put everything in order, both at home and away.

SPORTING ASSISTANCE

'Young men who pay rounds of visits to country houses cannot easily dispense with a valet.... Sportsmen, and men given to hunting and shooting, find the services of one invaluable' says *The Servants' Practical Guide.* **Out shooting he was required to be on hand to load his master's gun.**

Once his master had departed for his morning activities the valet busied himself folding away night clothes, clearing and cleaning the dressing stand, replacing used towels with clean ones and dusting the room. He needed to put out any clothes that might be required 'in case of a master's coming home wet from a ride'. Clothes for the evening including white tie for dinner were also prepared and laid out.

THE LADY'S MAID MUST ATTEND TO EVERYTHING REGARDING THE TOILETTE OF HER MISTRESS

ALL THE MOST INTIMATE FORMS OF ATTENTION, TO BOTH HER MISTRESS'S PERSON AND HER CLOTHES, WERE THE RESPONSIBILITY OF THE LADY'S MAID.

Several times a day the lady's maid was required to dress, undress and re-dress her mistress, as well as attending to her hair, but her first tasks each morning were to lay out her clothes (if this had not been done the night before), to make sure that she had hot water for washing and to check that the housemaid had laid the fire and attended to the dressing room. Once her mistress was dressed, and her hair combed and styled, she needed to put out any clothes for walking or riding and prepare garments for dinner in the evening.

THE ART OF DRESSING

In helping her mistress to dress, every detail needed attention. For instance, as Mrs Beeton says: *'Arrange the folds of the dress over the crinoline petticoats .... See that the sleeves fall well over the arms. If [the outfit] is finished with a jacket, or other upper dress, see that it fits smoothly under the arms, pull out the flounces and spread out the petticoat at the bottom with the hands, so that it falls in graceful folds. In arranging the petticoat itself, a careful lady's maid will see that this is firmly fastened around the waist.'*

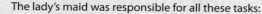
The lady's maid was responsible for all these tasks:
• Cleaning and mending clothes, and attention to millinery.
• Washing under garments, cleaning shoes.
• Assisting with undressing after dinner and evening entertainment.
• Helping her mistress into her night clothes.
• Ascertaining needs for the following day.
• Putting her mistress's jewellery safely away.
And …
• When a lady kept a dog it was the lady's maid's duty to attend to it, wash it and take it out for walks as necessary.

THE MISTRESS'S WARDROBE IS KEPT IN GOOD REPAIR BY HER MAID

CARING FOR HER MISTRESS'S CLOTHING WAS PARAMOUNT AMONG THE RESPONSIBILITIES OF THE LADY'S MAID.

During the winter and in wet weather, dresses needed to be carefully examined, and any mud removed. If made of tweed or some other woollen material they could be laid on a table and brushed all over, but for lighter fabrics it was better to beat them lightly with a handkerchief or thin cloth. Silk dresses were never brushed, but rubbed with a piece of merino, or other soft material of a similar colour, kept for the purpose. Summer dresses of barège (a sheer woven fabric of silk or cotton and wool), muslin, mohair, and other light materials, simply required shaking. If creased, muslin needed to be ironed.

A lady's maid was often required to be a dressmaker, at least for ordinary day wear. Evening gowns and the like were created for the mistress of the house and her daughters by professional dressmakers.

MILLINERY INSTRUCTIONS FROM MRS BEETON

'The bonnet should be dusted with a light feather plume, in order to remove every particle of dust …. Velvet bonnets, and other velvet articles of dress, should be cleaned with a soft brush. If the flowers with which the bonnet is decorated have been crushed or displaced, or the leaves tumbled, they should be raised and readjusted by means of flower-pliers. If feathers have suffered from damp, they should be laid near the fire for a few minutes, and restored to their natural state by the hand or a soft brush.'

THE CLEANEST LINEN

Removing unwanted stains and marks from delicate fabrics was a requisite skill for a good lady's maid. Some popular 19th-century treatments included:

- **Ink-spots:** pour on a few drops of hot water immediately after staining, then dip immediately in cold water.
- **Fruit stains on linen:** rub each side of the fabric with yellow soap, tie up a piece of pearlash (potassium carbonate) into the item and soak well or boil. Rinse and expose the stain to sun and air.
- **Grease stains:** pour some turpentine over the mark and rub until dry with a piece of clean flannel. Repeat as necessary, brush well and hang in the open air to remove the smell.
- **Wine stains on linen:** hold in boiling milk.

MAINTAINING LAMPS AND CANDLES IS A DAILY DUTY

DOZENS – IF NOT HUNDREDS – OF LAMPS AND CANDLES WERE NECESSARY TO LIGHT A LARGE COUNTRY HOUSE. THEIR DAILY SERVICING WAS THE SPECIALIST JOB OF LAMP AND CANDLEMEN.

Before the installation of electricity, a lamp room was generally set aside for storing and maintaining candles, candlesticks and a plethora of oil lamps. Each morning, lamps would be collected from the rooms of the house and their wicks checked. If necessary these were trimmed using scissors with blades fitted with circular lips to catch the residues and to prevent them from falling back into the lamps. From the 1850s, both colza oil (a type of rapeseed oil selected for its purity and pleasant smell) and paraffin were used for lamps and stored in large tanks in the lamp room.

Regular treatment

Each lamp needed to be taken apart at least once a week for cleaning the sooty glass and for the wicks to be trimmed. Metal globes and stands were also rubbed over and polished if necessary. Wicks had to be treated with great care daily to make them last as long as possible, while candlesticks – both simple designs and ornate candelabra – had to be carefully scraped in the lamp room to remove all remnants of dripped wax before being polished. To prevent lamps from smoking, soaking the wicks in strong vinegar then allowing them to dry was an effective remedy.

THE HOUSE MUST BE SET IN ORDER BEFORE STAFF RETIRE TO BED

A STRICT ROUTINE OF DUTIES WAS ESSENTIAL EVERY NIGHT TO MAKE SURE THAT THE HOUSE WAS PREPARED FOR THE FOLLOWING DAY AND ALSO KEPT SECURE.

Following dinner, tables were cleared by the footmen. Once washing up had been done, both cook and housekeeper needed to check that everything was in order before going to bed, with all dishes and cutlery put away. Making sure that all preserves were properly stored was the housekeeper's duty. Meanwhile, the scullery and lower housemaids might still be at work blacking the kitchen range and laying fires, while the lower footman or hallboy were filling coalscuttles and attending to lamps and candles.

For the valet, the day could not end until after his master had retired to bed and any clothes had been brushed by him personally or taken to the footman for attention. Similarly, the lady's maid was required to ensure that her mistress's evening dresses were properly hung up and any laundry removed for washing. If they had days off, lower servants had to be back in the house by 10 at night – or at an hour prescribed by the butler or housekeeper.

SAFE AND SECURE

Last to retire for the night was the butler. It was his duty to see that all the glasses and silver (the 'plate') were properly washed and dried, carried to the pantry and put away, the plate being kept under lock and key. His final task was to see that all the doors were locked and shutters drawn, and that any fires that had been alight during the evening had died down to a safe level.

THE
COUNTRY HOUSE
KITCHEN

The kitchen of the country house, and the many rooms attached to it for such specific purposes as making pastry, storing food and hanging game, was a hive of activity vital to the sustenance of family, staff and guests. In the earliest country houses the kitchen had a central position within the building but, as residences became larger and more complex in the late 17th century, it became separated from the main house and was provided with its own quarters.

The kitchen routine

By the Victorian era, with the burgeoning of technology, the kitchen had become what has been described as 'a complicated laboratory' with a vast range of equipment, all of which needed to be employed, cleaned and cared for by the team of kitchen staff, from the cook or chef to the lowly kitchen and scullery maids. However large the house and its staff, work in the kitchen took up almost every minute of the waking day, whether this was preparing meals for immediate consumption by employers and staff or for grand events planned into the calendar.

Home grown, home made

As far as possible, everything cooked in the country house kitchen had its origins on the estate, and menus were greatly governed by the seasons, although a great deal of food was preserved in some way for later use, especially the winter months. Where there were heated orangeries and greenhouses, exotic ingredients such as oranges and pineapples could also be supplied, and considered great luxuries. But whatever was cooked it was essential that the kitchen remained unobtrusive. It needed to run smoothly but, above all, be undetectable by sight, sound or smell by the family and their guests.

THE KITCHEN SHOULD NOT BE MADE OBVIOUS BY ITS ODOURS

A MAXIM DATING TO THE EARLY 20TH CENTURY WHEN COUNTRY HOUSE DESIGN BROUGHT THE KITCHEN AND DINING ROOM INTO CLOSER PROXIMITY.

In early country houses keeping the kitchen separate from the rest of the house was as much a precaution against fire as anything else, and by the 1680s, the trend was to separate the kitchen from the main block of the house into a separate pavilion, joined, as at Harleyford in Buckinghamshire, by an underground tunnel. This may have been inconvenient for serving meals, but was most satisfactory in removing odours. By Victorian times, the servant's wing of the largest houses had become so extensive that the kitchen was often far removed from the living quarters and had its own separate chimneys and vents. If on the same floor it was usually connected to the dining room by a long passageway deliberately designed to be devoid of any staircases up which odours could travel, or confined to the basement. The kitchen door might be covered with a heavy baize cloth to help keep odours confined.

MINIMIZING ODOURS

The country house cook was obliged to make sure that smells were minimized by ensuring that grease was not allowed to burn on the stove or in the oven and by putting a crust of bread into the water in which green vegetables were boiled. After being drained, the boiling liquid was then taken outside into the garden for disposal as soon as was practically possible.

The use of dustbins was specifically discouraged for their tendency to make a kitchen smell. Where pigs were kept on the estate, food waste was placed into pig bins for feeding these animals.

THE MAN COOK IS GENERALLY A FOREIGNER

WHILE MOST 'ORDINARY' COUNTRY HOUSES EMPLOYED WOMEN COOKS, FRENCH CHEFS WERE KEPT BY THE WEALTHIEST AND MOST PRESTIGIOUS FAMILIES.

If, in the 19th century, the man cook was an Englishman, it was said that he needed to be able to make the most fashionable foreign delicacies, which far outreached those of ordinary English cooking in their seasoning and flavour. The foreign cook would, it was assumed, have no problem in creating such dishes. When a man cook was employed he often had his own room adjacent to the kitchen where he could compose menus and refer to his collection of recipes in quiet and comfort.

Such was the status of the man cook that women aspiring to be heads of kitchens in the largest establishments needed to have experience of working as a man cook's assistant. In 1777, for example, a female cook seeking employment was careful to stress that she had been 'brought up under a man cook'.

A WEALTH OF EXPERIENCE
Whether male or female the cook needed experience and know how. In *The Servants Book of Knowledge* of 1773 Anthony Heasel stressed the importance, particularly for women, in the spheres of 'provisions in general, and also of the most proper methods used in dressing them'. Among the latter would have been the many French ways of preparing, cooking and serving dishes of all kinds.

A MULTITUDE OF DEMANDS

The many tasks of the ordinary country house cook are relayed in a poem of 1855 by Mark Forrester. The first lines of *'The Song of the Discontented Cook'* run:

Oh, who would wish to be a cook,
To live in such a broil!
With all one's pain, to cook one's brains,
And lead a life of toil?
'Tis, "Stir the pudding, Peggy,"
"And give those ducks a turn;
"Be quick, be quick, you lazy jade!
Else one or both will burn".'

But even when she was engaged to head the kitchen, the female cook always rated below the housekeeper in rank.

Matters of temper

All head cooks held sway over the kitchen staff and many were as irascible as they were tyrannical. It was not unusual for them to quit their posts without notice in high dudgeon, so it was always in the mistress's interests to keep them as sweet as possible.

FOR THE COOK, AN HOUR LOST IN THE MORNING WILL KEEP HER TOILING ALL DAY

WISE WORDS FOR COUNTRY HOUSE COOKS WHO NEEDED TO BE EXTREMELY EFFICIENT IN EVERYTHING THEY DID, ESPECIALLY WHEN THE HOUSE WAS FULL OF VISITORS.

Although her assistants would rise before her, the cook needed to be up by seven in the morning at the very latest to ensure that everything was in order before staff breakfast. Early morning tea was made and brought to her by the kitchen maid. By 7.30 she needed to be ready to receive food deliveries from the gardener and local tradesmen.

Depending on produce available, the cook then finalized the day's menus, which she would present to her mistress following family breakfast, making any adjustments afterwards according to activities organized for the day and the needs of any guests. These meetings were also used as an opportunity for planning large dinners, ball suppers and the like in advance.

The baking routine

Following the preparation and serving of lunch, cake baking, both for tea and for the day ahead, (and more for fruit cakes needing time to mature) was an afternoon activity, as were time consuming activities such as making gelatine. But serving dinner on time, and to the required standard, was the cook's major preoccupation. Not only were there four or more courses to be prepared, but there might be six or eight different choices for each (see box overleaf). The height of activity was from about six in the evening to the serving of the last course of dinner at nine or later. Only when everything had been cleared and the kitchen cleaned and made ready for the next day could the cook retire to bed.

THE FRUITS OF EXPERIENCE

Despite the appearance of cookery books such as those written by Eliza Acton and Mrs Beeton, most country house cooks rarely consulted recipes but carried the knowledge of everything they cooked – and the quantities required – in their heads as a result of years of experience.

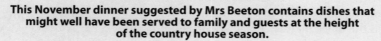

This November dinner suggested by Mrs Beeton contains dishes that might well have been served to family and guests at the height of the country house season.

Ox-tail soup
Soup à la Jardinière
— • —
Turbot and Lobster Sauce
Crimped Cod and Oyster Sauce

Stewed Eels
Soles à la Normandie

Pike and Cream Sauce
Fried Filleted Soles
— • —
Filets de Boeuf à la Jardinière

Croquettes of Game aux Champignons

Chicken Cutlets
Mutton Cutlets and Tomato Sauce

Lobster Rissoles Oyster Patties

Partridge aux fines herbes
Larded Sweetbreads

Roast Beef
Poulets aux Cressons

Haunch of Mutton Roast Turkey

Boiled Turkey and Celery Sauce
Ham
— • —
Grouse Pheasants Hare

Salad Artichokes Stewed Celery

Italian Cream
Charlotte aux Pommes
Compôte of Pears

Croûtes madrées aux Fruits
Pastry Punch Jelly

Iced Pudding
— • —
Desserts and Ices

COPPER POTS ARE KITCHEN ESSENTIALS

THE DURABILITY AND RELIABILITY OF COPPER POTS, SUPERB AT CONDUCTING HEAT, MADE THEM VITAL EQUIPMENT IN THE COUNTRY HOUSE KITCHEN.

Copper in the kitchen was only totally safe to use when coated inside with a thin layer of tin. Without such a precaution there was a strong risk of verdigris poisoning, which resulted from the contamination of food with the copper oxides. For this reason the cook and her underlings all needed to keep a close eye on the scrupulous cleanliness of unlined copper utensils and their linings as Mrs Beeton explains (see Taking care of copper). Copper also needed meticulous daily cleaning using rotten-stone, a very fine abrasive powder, mixed with soft soap and oil of turpentine to a stiff putty.

Not only does copper conduct heat extremely well but was particularly prized by country house cooks, like those of today, for whisking egg whites. When beaten in a copper bowl, the foam not only takes on a creamy yellow colour but retains the stiffness essential for making confections such as meringues and soufflés.

Copper on show

Original copper pots and pans are on display in many kitchens of country houses open to visit. One particularly excellent collection can be seen at the Regency masterpiece of Saltram House in Devon which, as well as saucepans and frying pans, includes a wide range of kettles, teapots, bakeware, jelly moulds and serving utensils, many of them beautifully ornate.

The largest utensils

As well as being used for preparing and cooking food, 'coppers' were also large vessels or boilers in which water was heated in the scullery on a gas burner. These were regularly used for scalding cloths and, in the largest houses, for cooking vegetables.

TAKING CARE WITH COPPER

Mrs Beeton was in no doubt about the importance of using copper utensils safely. *'Copper utensils should never be used in the kitchen unless time, and the utmost care should be taken, not to let the tin be rubbed off. If by chance this should occur, have it replaced before the vessel is again brought into use. Neither soup nor gravy should, at any time, be suffered to remain in them longer than is absolutely necessary, as any fat or acid that is in them, may affect the metal, so as to impregnate with poison what is intended to be eaten.'*

FOR HER PASTRY THE COOK SHOULD HAVE A THICK BOARD IN WINTERTIME AND A MARBLE SLAB FOR SUMMER USE

EXCELLENT ADVICE FOR ANY COUNTRY HOUSE PASTRY
COOK STRIVING FOR PERFECTION WITH HER BAKING.

Pastry became an edible ingredient from Tudor times
– before that it was a thick and tough mixture of flour
and water used to enclose and seal the contents of pies
before being discarded. Once it became edible and finer,
with eggs and fat such as butter and suet added, coolness
became vital. Both types of board would have been readily
available in the country house pastry room – a separate
north-facing space adjacent to the kitchen designed
for coolness and unaffected by the heat from the
kitchen range.

Marble slabs were often set into tables in the
pastry room around whose walls were wooden
cupboards for storing ingredients; beneath the
pastry tables were storage areas for flour bins,

A DELICIOUS EXCEPTION

The exception to the 'cool rule' was the hot water pastry, still used today for pork
pies and made by melting lard in hot water then pouring it onto the flour. The
paste is then quickly rolled out or shaped by hand, either to line the sides of a
mould or to create the bottom and sides of the pie, which are then filled before
a pastry lid is added. The most elaborate pastry moulds, now collectors' items,
created pretty imprints of flowers and foliage on the finished items.

As *Cassell's Household Guide* instructs on pastry making: '*The temperature, i.e., consistence, of the butter is of considerable importance. Too hard, it will not easily mix with the flour; in a running state it will leak out at the edges in every roll. In winter, butter is easily warmed; in summer it may be plunged in cold pump water. Some cooks use ice.'*

wooden pastry boards and baking trays. Set-in drawers held rolling pins and other utensils. Although the pastry room was cool it was very often damp, so the flour was often sifted and set beside the fire to dry ahead of pastry making.

Mixing and shaping

Before being dusted with flour from a copper, brass or tinplate dredger, and rolled out with pins made of sycamore, or beech, pastry was mixed in large pottery bowls. It was trimmed into shape with a knife or, from the 16th century, with a pastry jagger or jagging iron, a gadget with a small spoon at one end and a cutting wheel at the other, a design that persisted for centuries.

THE STOCKPOT IS THE BASIS OF THE KITCHEN

STOCKPOTS, KEPT CONSTANTLY ON THE BOIL, WERE A STARTING POINT FOR ALMOST EVERY SAVOURY CREATION, FROM SOUPS TO GRAVIES AND GLAZES.

The traditional stockpot was a large, lidded pot, sometimes with a tap at the base for releasing liquid. In a large country house kitchen there would be two pots, one brown, one white, for brown and white soups and sauces. Bones always formed the basis of the stockpot – roasted beef bones for brown stock, veal bones and chicken carcasses for white.

Other ingredients included meat of various kinds, onions (with skins left on for brown stock), plus chopped carrots, celery, turnips, leeks or other vegetables to hand. Herbs such as bay, parsley and thyme were also added plus salt, pepper and, if desired, cloves and mace.

A constant duty

Skimming the stock of fat while it was bubbling gently was a constant duty for the kitchen maids. At around nine in the evening the stockpots would be taken off the range and the contents strained through hair sieves to remove every possible particle of grease. Next morning they would be brought back to the boil and more pieces of meat and vegetables added.

SHEER PERFECTION

To quote Mrs Beeton:
'It is on a good stock, or first good broth and sauce, that excellence in cookery depends. If the preparation of this basis of the culinary art is intrusted to negligent or ignorant persons, and the stock is not well skimmed, but indifferent results will be obtained.'

THE GREATEST POSSIBLE ATTENTION MUST BE PAID TO MAKING BUTTER

FOR BUTTER, FINE JUDGEMENT WAS NEEDED AT EVERY STAGE. MOST CRITICAL WAS TO ENSURE THAT IT WOULD SET OR 'COME', AN OPERATION OFTEN ACCOMPANIED BY THE USE OF CHARMS.

Milk for butter making was delivered from the home farm on the country house estate or provided by the cows that the dairymaid milked herself. For a large establishment, butter was made every day in summer when the cows were in full milk, and every two or three days at other times of the year.

First the cream was separated off by leaving the milk in wide pans for 24 hours, then skimmed using a skimming dish. After being left for two or three days to 'ripen' the milk was either rotated steadily or agitated with a plunger in a churn. Once the butter had 'come', the liquid buttermilk was poured off (to be fed to the pigs).

Well washed

Next the butter was transferred to shallow wooden tubs or bowls full of cold water – ideally

Speed and safety

To speed butter making, the cream might be taken off the milk before churning, and scalded to prevent it from becoming contaminated with microorganisms. Once made, the butter was shaped with wooden pats known as butlets or 'Scotch hands', or pressed into a variety of fancy moulds.

Since Satan or witches were thought to prevent butter from 'coming', to ward off their ill effects dairymaids would throw silver sixpences into the churn, hang stones with holes in them in the dairy and strew the floor with protective herbs including betony, clover, dill and St John's wort.

pure spring water – in which it was squeezed and washed by hand. Several washings were necessary before the water was clear, salt being added towards the end of this process. The final washing might be made in a butter worker, a shallow wooden tray fitted with rollers to mash its contents.

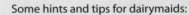

BETTER BUTTER

Some hints and tips for dairymaids:
• Hands must be clean and all utensils sterilized by scalding them with boiling water.
• Avoid rapid motion of the churn – it will force too much air into the butter and make it swell.
• Any milk spilt on the floor should be immediately cleaned up with boiling water.
• If butter refuses to 'come', wrap the cream in a calico cloth and leave it to drip for several days to make cream cheese.
• To prevent summer-made butter from going rancid, put it in a stoneware jar on a layer of crushed salt and top with more salt.

MEAT MUST BE TURNED WHILE ROASTING OVER A BRISK FIRE

USEFUL ADVICE FOR ROASTING MEAT OVER AN OPEN FIRE
BEFORE THE ADVENT OF THE KITCHEN RANGE.

Before the 18th century, meat was simply roasted by putting it on a spit and turning over a log fire, which might be raised up on a hearth within the fireplace. The spits were turned by hand, and sometimes even by dogs that ran on a kind of treadmill. For human servants it was hard, hot and thirsty work, but was eventually superseded, from the 16th century with a clockwork 'jack' driven by weights. Underneath the spits were lipped trays or dripping pans for catching fat and cooking juices, which could be ladled back over the meat to baste it.

THE IDEAL FIRE

A fire clear at the bottom, glowing and burning briskly was essential for a good roast. The Regency guide, *The Complete Servant* also said that: *'The ashes should be taken up, and the hearth made quite clean, before you begin to roast. If the fire requires to be stirred during the operation the dripping pan must be drawn back, so that then, and at all times, it may be kept clean from cinders and dust. Hot cinders, or live coals dropping into the pan make the dripping rank and spoil it for basting.'*

Beef, always a favourite meat in Britain, demanded special care. If it had been hung for some time it would need to be trimmed, soaked in salt water and dredged with flour

before cooking, and basted continually with dripping whilst roasting. It always lost about a third of its weight during cooking. Pork needed to be basted with salt and water and more thoroughly done compared with beef and lamb. After some time on the fire the skin was scored with a sharp knife to ensure good crackling.

A BREAD TROUGH SHOULD NEVER BE WASHED

VITAL ADVICE, NEEDED TO KEEP THE TROUGH IMPREGNATED WITH FERMENTED YEAST AND TO ENSURE THAT THE PREPARED DOUGH WOULD RISE RELIABLY TIME AFTER TIME.

The kneading trough was a thick, slanting wooden or slate container in which dough was mixed and was, from medieval times, key equipment in the bakehouse – a separate room often adjoining the brewhouse. Instead of being washed it was rubbed clean with a ball of dough.

In a large house bread was baked every day, in smaller ones several times a week, depending on the number of

Bakehouses and beyond

At Ingatestone Hall in Essex in the mid 16th century, three kinds of bread were made – fine white bread or 'manchet', and two types of wholemeal bread, the one intended for the servants being the coarser. Lanhydrock in Cornwall still has a typical dry, warm bakehouse.

With the introduction of kitchen ranges, old style bakehouses became less common. Instead, bread was made in the kitchen or an attached baking scullery, and baked in tins rather than hand shaped loaves.

occupants. The process began in the evening when flour was mixed with water and yeast, kneaded and left to rise overnight in the baking trough, covered with a wooden lid and warm sacks. The top of the lid, usually removable, was handy for shaping and moulding the dough before its final rising or 'proving'. A plain round loaf was finished by slashing a cross into the top to ensure perfect rising (and supposedly to keep out the Devil). When not in use, the kneading trough was used for storing baking tins, cloths and small quantities of flour.

Heat for baking

On a baking day brick-built or lined ovens were lit in the morning, two or three hours ahead of use. The oldest country house oven was the beehive (named from its shape). Dry, fast-burning wood such as furze and blackthorn faggots that heated the bricks thoroughly to a high temperature were essential. Dough was inserted into the oven on a peel – a pole with a wide blade at one end – but only after the ashes and embers had been removed from the oven base and the cavity cleaned with a barely wrung wet cloth.

A WHOLE FISH IS BEST COOKED IN A KETTLE

FISH KETTLES WERE ESSENTIALS OF THE COUNTRY HOUSE COOK'S BATTERIE DE CUISINE AND ALSO USED TO COOK SHELLFISH RANGING FROM LOBSTERS TO COCKLES.

The original fish kettles were made of iron, which was succeeded by brass followed, from the mid 18th century onward, by copper, which became the kitchen standard. For cooking a fish the kettle would be set on iron trivets placed on the stove.

In a kettle, fish was usually cooked in a *court bouillon* – water with lemon or vinegar and herbs added, although Izaak Walton (1593–1683), author of *The Compleat Angler*, recommended stale beer and a flavouring of horseradish in addition to the usual rosemary, thyme and winter savoury. For trout, he said, 'let your liqueur boil up to the height before you put in the fish; and then if there be many, put them in one by one, that they may not cool the liquor as to make it fall.'

Before being simmered in the kettle, fish was kept in the same larder as meat on a purpose-made slab where it could be immersed in a continuous stream of cold water.

PERFECTLY FRESH

Eating the freshest fish from the estate was greatly valued, as Jane Loudon wrote in 1843: '... we had a dish of the finest carp or tench I ever met with, or probably a jack, or eels, each taken from the stew ponds immediately before dinner, and thus eaten in the highest perfection.' Even the garnish was home grown – watercress for perch and wild thyme for trout. But despite having a hunk of bread stuffed into the cavity left after the stomach had been removed, freshwater fish often tasted distinctly muddy.

Alternatively it might be laid on sacks filled with ice and placed in zinc-lined cupboard-like containers. Near the coast, or at houses with extensive fishing, there would be a separate fish larder. Here, fish might even be kept alive, hung in a net filled with wet moss and fed with bread and milk in order to maximize their flavour.

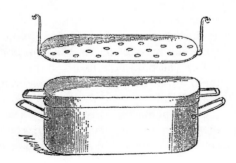

HANG GAME IN A CURRENT OF DRY AIR

HOUSES ON SUBSTANTIAL ESTATES HAD GAME LARDERS IN THE GROUNDS WHERE PERFECT VENTILATION COULD BE ENSURED AND THE EFFECTS OF UNPLEASANT ODOURS MINIMIZED.

The ideal game larder had large windows and plenty of air vents with a cool slate and/or stone floor. For hanging whole carcasses, such as venison, it had rails or substantial wooden beams, while for hanging game birds, and smaller items such as rabbits and hares, a tiered iron frame was suspended from the ceiling. Chopping slabs were provided for butchering. By the turn of the 20th century, small cooling plants – pipes filled with brine cooled with compressed carbon dioxide – were being installed for long-term storage.

Well hung

Before being cooked and eaten, venison was hung for at least two weeks, after which it was washed in milk and water before being dried with clean cloths.

BEST RESULTS

Good game birds needed to be fat. If stale, the skin would peel off when rubbed with the finger. Tough, old geese were betrayed by their red feet and yellow, skinny fat. Preparing game birds, which included quails, snipe, woodcock, plovers and even larks, was a time consuming business. As well as having to be plucked and gutted they needed to be stuffed (if large), trussed and, if likely to be dry, larded by having strips of fat sewn into the breast with a larding needle.

The designer larder

Elegant but efficient, the game larder designed by Humphrey Repton for Uppark in West Sussex in the early 19th century, is a perfect example. Octagonal in shape it is divided into two 'rooms', one for smaller game, the other for carcasses. Additional cool storage space is supplied by marble shelves placed in alcoves.

Any parts of the meat likely to be attacked by flies were rubbed with ground ginger or pepper. Good venison would have fat that was thick, clear and bright, not green or black. Hares were hung for a similar period before being 'jugged' with onions, herbs and possibly port added as well as some of the animal's own blood.

A COOK'S SAUCES MARK THE CREDIT OF HER KITCHEN

NOT ONLY THAT, BUT EACH SAUCE NEEDED TO HAVE ITS OWN CHARACTER, FITTED TO THE DISH IT ACCOMPANIED.

Making sauces was a preoccupation of the country house kitchen, particularly when catering for grand occasions and was usually the duty of the kitchen maid. For grand cooking between the 15th and 17th centuries the basis of a good sauce was the cullis, used for both thickening and flavouring. It was made with butter and breadcrumbs, which could be flavoured with truffles, crayfish or champagne.

For simpler everyday dishes thinner sauces made with butter and a little flour, plus cream or stock were used, flavoured with parsley, anchovies, shrimps and the like. These became the norm despite evoking the scorn of contemporary 'foodies' for their blandness and tendency to lumpiness.

SAUCE WITH CHARACTER

As Mrs Beeton prescribed, each sauce needed to *'possess a decided character; and whether sharp or sweet, savoury or plain, they should carry their names in a distinct manner ...'* **This included sauces such as mint, apple, gooseberry and onion as well as mayonnaise which by the mid 19th century was popular for cold dishes.**

The essential repertoire

Until the 1600s most sauces were strongly spiced with nutmeg and cloves. Often they would also contain ingredients such as raisins as well as lemon juice and vinegar or verjuice made from unripe grapes. By the late 18th century sauce was, in grand houses, always served separately in a sauce boat. Around 1800, thanks to the influence of French chefs such as Marie-Antoine Carême (1784 – 1833), three essential sauces had become established in the cook's repertoire: the béchamel, the velouté made with a light stock, and the éspagnole based on a brown stock.

GOOD GRAVY

To accompany roast meat gravy was essential. It could be made in two ways:

Using breadcrumb thickening: A recipe from *Enquire Within* of 1894 typifies the cullis method: 'Three onions sliced, and fried in butter to a nice brown; toast a large thin slice of bread until quite hard and of a deep brown. Take these, with any piece of meat, bone &c., and some herbs and set them on the fire, with water according to judgement, and stew down until a rich gravy is produced. Season, strain and keep cool.'

Using a roux: From *Cassell's Household Guide*, using gravy 'produced by the cooking of meat'. This is 'thickened, without being boiled down by the addition of various materials, such as a roux of flour and butter...' Alternative thickenings included the yolks of hard-boiled eggs and roasted chestnuts crushed to a powder. Good stock, or white or red wine, were all recommended additions.

THE TASK OF KEEPING FOOD HOT DESERVES CONSIDERABLE ATTENTION

THE GREATER THE DISTANCE BETWEEN KITCHEN AND
DINING ROOM, THE MORE DIFFICULT IT WAS TO KEEP
FOOD HOT. BOTH EQUIPMENT AND TIMING WERE
CRUCIAL.

For food to have a chance of being a good temperature
when it reached the table it needed to be piping hot
when it left the kitchen. All hot dishes were kept simmering
on the stove or left in the oven before being lifted onto
thoroughly heated serving dishes which were then quickly
covered with large metal domes – also heated. Plates, too,
had to be heated before being sent to the dining room. Soup
was sent up in a hot tureen to be ladelled into hot plates in
the dining room.

PLANNING AND TIMING

**Advising cooks on the importance of hot food, *The Complete Servant*
stressed that:**

*'... the clock must be consulted, and the different articles prepared and
laid to the fire, in succession, according to the times they will take, that
all may be ready in due time. A scene of activity now commences in
which you must necessarily be cool, collected and attentive. Have an
eye to the roast meat, and an ear to the boils, and let your thoughts
continually recur to the rudiments of your art, which at this moment
must be called into practical requisition. You will endeavour that every
vegetable, and of sauce, be made to keep pace with the dishes to which
they respectively belong – so that all may go upstairs smoking hot
together, and in due order.'*

To ensure perfect timing, cook and staff had to work in harmony. The butler was the essential go-between with the dining room and ideally advised, to the minute, when food should leave the kitchen. For breakfasts and informal suppers, food could be kept hot in a chafing dish. Traditionally made of silver it consisted of an outer container filled with water into which an inner pan containing the food was placed. The whole was heated from below with an oil or spirit lamp.

EVERY DISH SHOULD BE SENT TO THE TABLE PROPERLY GARNISHED

BY THE MID 19TH CENTURY, GARNISHING DISHES WAS NOT ONLY EXPECTED BUT HAD BECOME A CULINARY ART THAT TOOK UP CONSIDERABLE TIME IN THE COUNTRY HOUSE KITCHEN.

Such were the demands of good dining that the simple sprig of parsley, chervil or mint, or the finely chopped herb, was an inadequate garnish for any dish. For cold dishes, elaborately shaped decorations were made by cutting root vegetables such as carrot and turnips into floral shapes and leaving them in cold water to 'blossom', scooping out cucumber flesh into 'peas' and dicing artichoke hearts. Lemon and mushroom slices were also popular, as were cooked prawns and shrimps, which might also be added as decoration before serving soup.

THE EXPERT'S CHOICE

One of Mrs Marshall's more complex suggestions was a 'Reform Garnish' for cutlets or a braised fowl, which sound almost like a dish in itself: *'Take Julienne shreds of French gherkin, truffle, button mushroom, cooked ox tongue or ham, and hard boiled white of egg, making in all half a pint; put between two plates with a little white stock or water and boil over boiling water.'*

Cooked garnishes

For hot dishes, garnishes might well be cooked. Mrs Agnes B. Marshall recommended garnishes such as cucumber flesh cut into olive shapes boiled, then tossed in butter, lemon juice and parsley or button onions blanched and braised. To make the creation of small vegetable garnishes easier, cooks would use specifically fashioned implements such as pea-cutters and melon ballers.

ORNATE GARNISHES

For effect, garnishes like preserved cherries and other fruits, and crystallized flowers such as violets, were threaded onto ornate silver or silver-plated skewers known as *attelettes*. Most elaborate of all was spun sugar, which involved boiling sugar to a perfect 'crack stage' caramel (extremely difficult without the aid of a sugar thermometer) then using implements such as forks and spoons to 'throw' it over a rolling pin and draw it into fine threads.

MIXING THE SALAD IS THE DUTY OF THE BUTLER

ALTHOUGH USUALLY MADE BY THE COOK OR ONE OF HER ASSISTANTS, THE FINAL TOUCHES ADDED JUST BEFORE SERVING TO PREVENT LIMPNESS, WERE THE BUTLER'S RESPONSIBILITY.

Salads were generally supper dishes which, at their simplest, consisted of mixed green leaves such as lettuce, watercress, mustard and cress, but possibly also corn salad and sorrel. The country house salad might also contain young nettle and dandelion leaves and flowers such as nasturtiums. In winter, cabbage (commonly pickled) and shredded Brussels sprouts were used, as well as celery and chicory. Other common ingredients included beetroot, cucumber, radishes, spring onions and potatoes. Cooked carrots, cauliflower and French beans might be used too.

Extra touches

Among the many 'fancy salads' devised by the renowned cook Mrs Agnes B. Marshall were an Italian salad of cooked potatoes, cucumber, boiled cauliflower, artichoke hearts and Brussels sprouts in a dressing flavoured with tarragon, chervil and chopped shallots, garnished with anchovy-stuffed olives. Salad flavourings included chervil, mint, parsley, tarragon, sage and garlic. Tomatoes did not become a usual salad ingredient until the 19th century. Originally regarded with some suspicion, they were more likely to be served baked or as a flavouring for soups and gravies.

THE PERFECT DRESSING

Enquire Within amused and informed its readers with this ode entitled 'Salad Mixture in Verse'. The 'oil of Lucca' is Italian olive oil.

Two large potatoes, passed through kitchen sieve,
Unwonted softness to the salad give;
Of mordant mustard add a single spoon –
Distrust the condiment which bites so soon;
But deem it not thou man of herbs, a fault
To add a double quantity of salt;
Three times the spoon with oil of Lucca crown,
And once with vinegar procured from town.
True flavour needs it, and your pet begs
The pounded yellow of two well-boiled eggs;
Let onion atoms lurk within the bowl,
And, scarce suspected, animate the whole;
And lastly, on the favoured compound toss
A magic teaspoon of anchovy sauce;
And then, though green turtle fail, though venison's
  tough,
And ham and turkey be not boiled enough
Serenely full, the epicure may say, –
'Fate cannot harm me – I have dined today.'

SALADS WITH SUBSTANCE

For a more substantial dish, meat was added to a salad as in the popular Victorian 'Salmagundi' – a ring of blanched lettuce hearts filled with alternate circular layers of beetroot, egg yolks, watercress, egg whites, chopped cold meat and pickled cabbage. Seafood might be used instead of meat, and nuts added.

THE WET LARDER MUST CONTAIN EQUIPMENT FOR SALTING

BEFORE REFRIGERATION, PRESERVING MEAT WAS OF PRIMARY CONCERN AND WAS CARRIED OUT IN THE WET LARDER IN WHICH IT WAS TRADITIONALLY STORED.

As well as meat intended for long keeping, even fresh meat was rubbed with salt to help prevent it from becoming tainted, but before this it would always need scrutinizing to ensure that it was not afflicted with 'fly strike', that is, with eggs laid by houseflies and any suspicious lumps of fat – especially the gelatinous 'kernels' that might contain tape worms – cut off.

MAKING HAM AND BACON

As well as being salted, ham and bacon needed to be smoked, usually in a separate smoking room.

For ham: Rub the pork with a little salt and leave it overnight. Next day, boil together half a pound of bay (sea) salt, half a pound of common salt and half a pound of moist sugar with a quart of stale beer. Pour it over the meat and baste and turn it for three weeks. Dry the ham over a fire of wood, sawdust and peat.

For bacon: treat the meat as for ham, then roll it in bran before hanging it up to smoke. Or enclose it in a coarse cloth, sewing it in securely, then hang it for a week in a baker's chimney.

Salted over time

For longer preservation, a mixture of salt and saltpetre (potassium nitrate) was used, which was kept in a powdering tub, and meat placed on wooden trestles or on a salting stone or shallow sink in the larder. In addition, salting troughs might be placed around the larder, supported on bricks. Deep troughs were for long-term storage, shallow ones for more immediate use. Both were filled with a liquid pickling solution, typically containing salt and saltpetre plus sugar and flavourings such as bay leaves.

Alternatives to the troughs were lead-lined wooden tubs or large earthenware crocks. Meat could be left in them for up to 12 months, being periodically topped up with salt, but two to three weeks' steeping was more usual.

PRESERVES ARE THE HOUSEKEEPER'S PROVINCE

MAKING PICKLES, KETCHUPS, CHUTNEYS, JAMS, JELLIES AND MARMALADES, PLUS SYRUPS, DISTILLED WATERS, AND EVEN ESSENTIAL OILS AND COSMETICS, WERE IMPORTANT DUTIES FOR THE HOUSEKEEPER.

Making preserves took place in the stillroom, essentially a 'better kind of kitchen' used for storing all kinds of preserves as well as sugar, spices and other precious ingredients. with the assistance of one or more kitchen maids. All kinds of home-grown vegetables were pickled. Onions, beetroot and cabbage – both green and white – were favourites, along with green and red tomatoes. Unripe walnuts were also pickled in vinegar as were fruits of all kinds, including plums, peaches and, if they were grown in hothouses, lemons and oranges. Ketchups were made from everything from tomatoes to cucumbers and mushrooms and even oysters.

Vinegars were flavoured in the stillroom with anything from gooseberries, currants, horseradish, mint, chilli (see recipe overleaf) to elderflowers, roses and dried primrose petals. Curry powders were also mixed here, as were other powdered flavourings such as 'peas powder' made from a mixture of dried mint and sage, celery seed and either cayenne pepper or allspice.

Sugar treatment

Syrups for preserves were made using orange or lemon peel, and plain syrups used for preserving apples and other fruit, often with large amounts of brandy or other liqueur added. They were also used as the basis for sweet, flavoured drinks of all kinds. Rose petals, and whole flowers such as violets, were preserved by being crystallized. This was done by dipping them into a sugar syrup, or coating them in lightly whisked egg white before rolling them in crushed sugar.

KITCHEN-MADE TREATMENTS

'Beverages' for medicinal use were made in the stillroom, including potash water and liquid magnesia. For seltzer and soda waters, a forcing pump was used to add carbonic acid gas to the mixtures to make them fizz.

COUNTRY HOUSE KETCHUP

A recipe from Tendring Hall in Suffolk from 1857, quoted by
Florence White in her 1932 book *Good Things in England*.
NOTE: The final waste-saving tip is of most dubious safety! **On no
account do this at home.**

Ingredients: tomatoes, quite ripe; chilli vinegar, salt, garlic ½ oz; or
shallots 1 oz to each quart.
Time: bake for about 15 minutes; boil for 15.

Method
1. Bake quite ripe tomatoes till they are perfectly soft.
2. Rub the pulp through a sieve.
3. Add as much chilli vinegar as will make a fairly thick cream.
4. Slice the garlic or shallot and boil all together for 15 minutes.
5. Take the scum off.
6. Strain it through a sieve to remove the garlic or shallot.
7. When cold, bottle and cork it well.

N.B. – If when the bottles are opened it is found to have fermented, put
more salt to it and boil it up again. The thickness when finished should
be that of very thick cream.

Her other recipes include a cucumber ketchup flavoured with
ginger, pepper and mace, and a variety of pickles and chutneys
using ingredients such as rhubarb, beetroot, plums and peaches.

A POT OF HOME-MADE MARMALADE GIVES GREATEST ZEST TO THE APPETITE

MARMALADE, ONCE ADVERTISED AS 'THE ARISTOCRAT OF THE BREAKFAST TABLE' BECAME A COUNTRY HOUSE STAPLE IN THE 18TH CENTURY. SERVING READY-BOUGHT MARMALADE WOULD DEFINITELY HAVE BEEN FROWNED UPON.

Like other preserves marmalade, which could be made with lemons or limes as well as bitter Seville oranges was prepared in the stillroom. The best sugar, which in the 19th century was made into large 'loaves' weighing anything from 5 to 35 lb (2.5 to 17.5 kilos) after being refined, was expensive but essential to the making of good marmalade and needed to be broken up by hand, using large choppers or smaller 'nippers' before it could be used.

The word 'marmalade' also refers to the stiff set or moulded preserves made from quinces and other fruits such as damsons, apples and pears. Traditionally these were served as elements of desserts.

A DELICIOUS REMEDY

When citrus fruits were first made into marmalade in the 1600s the resulting concoction was used as a remedy for indigestion. Only in the early 18th century after Janet, wife of James Keiller of Dundee, made them into a jam to allay their bitterness was breakfast marmalade 'invented'.

As today, marmalade making took place in late winter or early spring when Seville oranges are at the best and most readily available. Recipes such as this one from 1896, which involves no straining through muslin, will probably produce a quite cloudy but still tasty result.

Take the twenty four large Seville oranges, and double their
weight in loaf sugar.
Wash and rub the oranges well in cold water, to clean them.
Put them in a pan with enough cold water to flat them and boil them
till the rinds are soft enough to be easily pierced with a pin.
Then drain off all the water, cut each orange in quarters,
and remove all the pips.
Put these pips into a basin, with one pint of cold water, and let
them stand twelve hours.
Next, remove all the pulp from the oranges and put it into another
basin, mash it well with a fork to prevent it being in lumps.
Now scrape the empty skins of the oranges till they are quite clean,
and slice them as thinly and evenly as possible.
Then drain off the water from the pips on to the loaf sugar,
and add the juice of six large lemons.
Boil this syrup till it is as thick as oil; stir well, then add the orange
pulp and cut-up rinds, and boil gently till it jellies when a few drops
are cooled on a plate.
It will probably take about half an hour. Put it in jars.
When cold, tie down tightly.

SAVOURIES ARE SERVED AT BOTH LARGE AND SMALL DINNERS

ESPECIALLY POPULAR IN VICTORIAN TIMES – AND WITH MALE DINERS – SAVOURIES WERE SERVED AFTER SWEET DISHES AND BEFORE ICES. AT SMALLER DINNERS THEY MIGHT BE SERVED AS AN ALTERNATIVE TO SWEET DISHES.

True to their name, savouries were well flavoured, and often served on toast, although they could contain sweet elements such as prunes and raisins. Marinated herring, anchovies and devilled shrimps were regularly employed. A typical topping, in an era when oysters were cheap and plentiful, was an oyster sauce made with fresh oysters flavoured with lemon juice, cayenne and salt. Savouries that involved setting ingredients such as caviare and lobster in aspic, were often served in paper cases. Or small pastry cases or profiteroles might be filled with a cheese mixture.

SWEET AND SPICY
Devilled muscatel raisins, deep fried then seasoned with salt, paprika (known as coralline pepper from its colour) and ground ginger were a variety of fruit-based savoury.

A MATTER OF MANNERS

Obeying the rules of etiquette was absolutely vital to the smooth running of the country house. The key was to make sure that everyone was comfortable in their position and that the essential barriers between 'upstairs' and 'downstairs' remained intact. While the nuances of family behaviour were laid down by the master and mistress, servants needed to know how to address and care for everyone in the household, whether serving food and wine at meals, running a bath or meeting guests at the station.

Rules for guests

For guests, knowing the rules was even more vital, for it was incredibly easy to offend unintentionally with the wrong dress, speech or action. The good hostess would, of course, inform her guests ahead of a visit about any activities that would demand particular modes of dress, but it was incumbent on guests to know the 'form' – and stick to it come what may. The same applied to servants such as ladies' maids and valets accompanying their masters and mistresses on country house visits. Discretion was also crucial. To discuss the business of the house with strangers was always unacceptable.

Orders of precedence

Throughout the house, orders of precedence prevailed and needed to be adhered to strictly. This not only involved knowing whose orders needed to be obeyed but also which parts of the house were out of bounds, even within the confines of the servants' quarters. For family and guests, rank and age needed to be taken into consideration and for unmarried girls chaperones were always on hand, although for the determined there were always means of escaping close supervision.

EVERYONE IN THE HOUSEHOLD MUST BE CORRECTLY ADDRESSED

IT WAS AS IMPORTANT FOR STAFF TO BE PROPERLY ADDRESSED BY THEIR EMPLOYERS AS IT WAS FOR STAFF TO CONVERSE CORRECTLY WITH MEMBERS OF THE HOUSEHOLD.

Forms of address depended largely on staff seniority. House steward, butler and valet were addressed by their surnames, while the housekeeper was always given the title of 'Missus', even if she was unmarried. Similarly, a cook was always 'Mrs', but if a 'man cook' was kept he was known as 'Monsieur' (since he was usually French). A governess was always 'Miss', as was a lady's maid, but the latter could also

Extensions of the family

Servants of long standing were held in such regard that masters of the house might consider men servants their friends, and kindly mistresses put themselves out to care for staff who fell ill. Sir John Boileau, master of Ketteringham in Norfolk from 1836 declared that his servants 'were as much part of his family as his children'.

TAKING CARE

The conventions surrounding names helped to guard against over confidentiality. While employers were warned against adopting 'an arbitrary or haughty demeanour' and to inspire confidence in their staff, a caring attitude needed to fall short of the over familiarity that might breed idle gossip.

be addressed simply by her surname or first name – either was acceptable.

'Lower order' servants would address their superiors such as the butler, housekeeper and cook in the same way. But for them, even their given names might not be acceptable for general use. They would either be called by their surnames or, if first names were used, had to answer to names ascribed by their employers. James and John were popular for footmen and Emma for housemaids. Emily, Jane and Mary were also regularly used for female servants. Any unusual given name – even Ada or Marion – would commonly be banned as pretentious.

A LADY'S DRESS MUST BE ADAPTED TO CIRCUMSTANCES AND VARIED WITH DIFFERENT OCCASIONS

BEING CORRECTLY DRESSED AT ALL TIMES WAS A PRIORITY FOR THE MISTRESS OF THE COUNTRY HOUSE AND HER DAUGHTERS, ASSISTED BY THEIR LADIES' MAIDS.

Several changes of dress were required each day – and more if sporting activities such as hunting were enjoyed. To start the day, the country house mistresses would wear simple morning dresses. Later in the morning, if going out walking they might, in the Edwardian era, change into a walking skirt and blouse, possibly a *trotteuse* skirt that

FOR A GRAND OCCASION

Dinner, or an occasion such as a ball, required something altogether grander. Advising its readers on dress for autumn country house parties of the early 1900s *The Lady's Realm* suggested: '*The stiffest velvets and brocades of the Louis XVI period, with decoration such as family lace falling over the décolletage.'* For young women it recommended a satin gown lined with soft muslin and with a bodice '*softened by a chemisette of thin frills of Indian muslin or chiffon'*.

cleared the ground but was shorter at the back than at the front. A matching coat would be worn, and possibly a waistcoat. Neat, smart footwear was a must.

To fit the event

For morning calls, yet another change was required, but as Mrs Beeton warned: 'Anything approaching evening dress is very much out of place.' For a visit of condolence it was appropriate to dress in black. Any outing away from the confines of the house demanded a hat as well as outerwear of some kind such as a cape or coat and, in winter a fur wrap. For afternoon wear a tea gown was also appropriate which, said the magazine *The Lady's Realm*, 'must be of good fabric' if it is to 'fall well'. This might be made of satin or silk, veiled with silk or lace.

STAFF CHANGES

Changes of dress were essential for some female servants, too. Housemaids, for instance, wore print dresses for their morning work then, following luncheon, changed into dark ones, topped with a frilly cap and apron.

WHEN RECEIVING CALLS, ETIQUETTE MUST BE GIVEN PROPER ATTENTION

THE WELCOMING OF VISITORS MAKING CALLS DEMANDED
CORRECT BEHAVIOUR FROM BOTH STAFF AND THE
MISTRESS OF THE HOUSE.

'There is no surer indication of the manner in which a household is conducted' says *The Servants' Practical Guide* of 1880, 'than is conveyed in "answering the door"'. The footman was instructed to open the hall door wide and to stand in the centre of the doorway before receiving cards from the visitors and, if the lady of the house was 'at home', (that is not only in residence but prepared to receive visitors) usher the visitors towards the drawing room. At the drawing room door the footman opened the door wide and announced 'Mrs A', 'Lady Emma F' or 'The Duke and Duchess of M', according to their position in society, correct wording being obligatory.

CARRY ON SEWING

When visitors arrived, counselled Mrs Beeton, *'Occupations such as drawing, music or reading should be suspended'.* **But if, she says, a lady is** *'engaged with light needlework, and none other is appropriate in the drawing-room, it may not be, under some circumstances, inconsistent with good breeding to quietly continue it during conversation, particularly if the visit be protracted, or the visitors be gentlemen.'*

Formalities of business

For business calls, the etiquette was slightly different, with visitors being asked to take a seat in the hall. The footman, having ascertained the nature of the call, would then take the visitor's card and either present it to his mistress on a salver or give it to her lady's maid for presentation. If taking the card to her himself he would, correctly, say: 'A person has called to see you, please ma'am and is waiting in that hall.' Or, 'A lady wishes to know if you will see her for five minutes, and has sent up her card, if you please ma'am.'

BIDDING FAREWELL

When she judged that a visit had come to an end the mistress of the house was advised to ring a bell for the footman then accompany her guests 'as far towards the door as the circumstances of your friendship seem to demand'.

FOR A COUNTRY HOUSE VISIT IT IS ALWAYS NECESSARY TO SELECT CORRECT AND SUITABLE CLOTHING

BEING PROPERLY DRESSED FOR EVERY OCCASION WAS ESSENTIAL FOR GUESTS, AND NEEDED TO COVER EVERYTHING FROM RIDING AND WALKING TO FORMAL DINING.

The fact that the country house 'season' took place in cooler months was reflected in the advice available for women which listed warm clothes of all kinds, as well as suitable indoor wear. Low, brogued shoes and woollen stockings were needed for traversing the moors, plus scarves and 'close fitting little hats' for warmth. For later in the day two or three simple evening gowns were recommended, depending on the length of the visit.

The male 'uniform'

For men, tweeds were essential for outdoor pursuits, in a weight fitted to the activity and the weather, and specifically tailored for activities such as shooting. Lighter wear was needed for tennis or croquet, and from the 1880s a blazer was acceptable for outdoor summer occasions. For

---

ESSENTIAL ACCESSORIES
For a formal dinner party, wearing good jewellery was not merely acceptable but expected, particularly for married women.

THE ALL PURPOSE WARDROBE

Advice from one Edwardian manual read: 'If she rides or hunts the girl must, of course, have the requisite kit. Otherwise she must have a tweed suit with a couple of woollen jumpers, a fur or other overcoat to wear over it in motoring, possibly a second tailor-made, and a simple day or a tea frock into which to slip when coming in from the hunt, or tramp, or motor run, to tea.'

more formal occasions a morning suit and dark waistcoat were needed for daytime wear and a tailcoat and white tie for dining. Trousers were loose and tubular cut and, from the mid 19th century, extended to meet the shoes. Cane, gloves and hat were obligatory accessories.

UNTIL LUNCHEON, VISITORS AT A COUNTRY HOUSE SHOULD LOOK ABOUT AND AMUSE THEMSELVES

POLITE COUNTRY HOUSE VISITORS WERE EXPECTED TO ARRANGE THEIR OWN MORNING ENTERTAINMENT UNLESS SOME PRE-PLANNED OUTING OR ACTIVITY WAS ORGANIZED FOR THEM.

Walking in the gardens or countryside would have been considered totally acceptable pre-luncheon activities for guests, as would driving out in a carriage or, later, a

---

ON THE ROAD

For motoring, which was the province of the wealthy until after World War II, the tailored suit was ideal. Hats were a must and, for women, tied with a fetching chiffon scarf over the top to keep them in place in open-topped vehicles.

---

motor car. Once cycling became fashionable and acceptable for both men and women in the 1880s, bicycle rides became another possible morning activity and a good host and hostess might provide machines for guests to use.

Designed for cycling

Cycling costumes were specifically designed for the activity, the women's magazine *Home Chat* of 1896 recommended those from Nicoll in London's Regent Street (the precursor of Harvey Nicholls), a store patronized, it assured its readers, by the Royal Family. 'A soft, light cloth should be chosen' it said, and 'A well-cut Norfolk jacket, a bright tie and a wide-sailor hat with riband to match combines comfort and shade.'

CYCLING FOR WOMEN

By 1904 *The Lady's Realm* **said that** *'the skirt for cycling should have an inverted pleat at the back, so that it falls on either side of the saddle... Tweed or a hard-wearing blue serge is always the most serviceable fabric.'*

THE ETIQUETTE OF SHOOTING IS MORE EASILY ACQUIRED THAN THE ART

KNOWING HOW TO BEHAVE WAS CRUCIAL TO THE SUCCESS AND SAFETY OF A SHOOTING PARTY, PARTICULARLY FOR COUNTRY HOUSE GUESTS.

On arrival for a shooting party, good guests would take their guns and cartridge bag to the gun room for safe keeping or, for a shoot on a grouse moor, leave them in the care of the keeper. To prepare for a day's shooting of birds including grouse, pheasant, duck and partridge, both landowner and male guests or 'guns' dressed in 'uniform' tweeds complete with Norfolk jackets whose full sleeves did not restrict the arms as the gun was raised, and a hat of some kind such as a deerstalker or tweed cap. Such clothes were essential for both warmth and camouflage.

Women usually joined the shoot for luncheon and to accompany the guns in the afternoon. Etiquette advice on dress included: 'Do not wear a loose fur or scarf or other conspicuous article of clothing that may be a disturbing element in a "drive".'

The duties of the host

Before the shoot began the correct host would ensure that everyone in the party knew the rules for the day such as 'no ground game' or 'no woodcock'. Until the shoot began, guns would be carried uncocked and cartridges secured in a shoulder bag. Out in the field, the 'guns' were placed at numbered stakes set in the ground at each site or 'drive' and took aim as the birds were driven overhead. The good host ensured that positions were rotated to give everyone a fair chance.

ADVICE IN VERSE

In 1902 the sportsman and army officer Mark
Beaufoy wrote a poem entitled *'A Father's Advice'*
which sums up the manners of the shoot:

If a sportsman true you'd be
Listen carefully to me. . .

Never, never let your gun
Pointed be at anyone.
That it may unloaded be
Matters not the least to me.

When a hedge or fence you cross
Though of time it cause a loss
From your gun the cartridge take
For the greater safety's sake.

If twixt you and neighbouring gun
Bird shall fly or beast may run
Let this maxim ere be thine
'Follow not across the line.'

Stops and beaters oft unseen
Lurk behind some leafy screen.
Calm and steady always be
'Never shoot where you can't see.'

You may kill or you may miss
But at all times think this:
'All the pheasants ever bred
Won't repay for one man dead.'

During a shoot it was considered poor form to pass across another man's sight, or to cross a neighbour's field to get to a wounded bird. Anyone attending a shoot but not a 'gun' needed to keep quiet except whilst walking between drives.

At the shoot's end, it was considered vulgar to announce how many birds you had bagged unless specifically asked to do so by the host. House guests then paid their required fee to the gamekeeper (as agreed with their host) and took their guns to the gun room to be cleaned. Anyone wishing to clean their own gun needed to be granted permission to do so ahead of their visit.

The language of the hunt

Knowing the language was vital. Hounds – never, ever, referred to as 'dogs' – were cast or let into coverts, rough brush areas of undergrowth where foxes often lie in hiding during the day. Once the hounds pick up the scent of a fox, they give tongue. Either the fox will go to ground or find shelter in an underground den or the hounds will exhaust and overtake him in a kill.

IF COMMISSIONED TO TAKE CHARGE OF A LADY IN THE HUNTING FIELD A MAN MUST SACRIFICE HIS SPORTING INSTINCTS TO A CERTAIN EXTENT

EQUALLY, SO 'MADGE OF TRUTH' ADVISED IN HER 1898 BOOK, HE MUST 'SEE HER SAFE OVER THE FENCES AND GIVE HER A LEAD 'AS CIRCUMSTANCES MAY DICTATE'.

As with shooting, hunting demanded meticulous attention to manners by everyone involved. A woman accompanied by a male rider was advised to follow closely, but not too close and to be aware of her position in the field at all times.

Dressing correctly was vital. Even if entitled to wear 'the pink' (a red hunting jacket) on his own territory, no good guest would don anything but a black jacket, white breeches and a velvet or silk hat. For women the 'uniform' was a long black skirt, tight fitting black jacket, stock (a scarf-like item) and a hat that could be completed with a veil or chiffon streamers. In the field any well mannered man was careful not to outrun or upstage the Master of Foxhounds and rewarded the groom who had charge of his hunter a generous tip.

A SAFE PARTNERSHIP

The author Anthony Trollope (1815 – 82), describing the hunting exploits of Lizzie and Lord George in 1872 advises Lizzie: *'When the men see that I am giving you a lead, they won't come between. If you hang back, I'll not go ahead. Just check your horse as he comes to his fences, and, if you can, see me over before you go at them.'* **Later in the piece Trollope tells us that he let her** *'... take the leap before he took it, knowing that, if there were misfortune, he might so best render help.'*

ONCE MADE, AN ENGAGEMENT AT A BALL SHOULD ON NO ACCOUNT BE BROKEN

GOOD MANNERS AT A BALL WERE PARAMOUNT, FROM SENDING TIMELY INVITATIONS TO CALLING ON THE HOST AND HOSTESS – OR LEAVING A CARD – WITHIN TWO OR THREE DAYS AFTERWARDS.

Dancing at a country house ball was opened by the mistress of the house or by the master and the lady of highest rank. During the ball, ladies had their dance cards filled by male partners. If breaking any 'engagement' was unavoidable, then it was polite for neither party to take part in that particular number. 'If, for instance,' one Victorian guide stated, 'two partners should claim one lady for the same quadrille or valse, the lady, having inadvertently engaged herself to both, should decline dancing with either, but should set the gentleman free to choose other partners.'

THE FIRST DANCE

By the mid 19th century the quadrille was the dance of choice to begin a ball but, said Mrs Beeton: *'It will be well for the hostess, even if she be very partial to the amusement, and a graceful dancer, not to participate in it to any great extent, lest her lady guests should have occasion to complain of her monopoly of the gentlemen, and other causes of neglect.'*

Before requesting a dance with a lady to whom he had not been introduced a polite gentleman would need to ask his host or hostess, or a member of the family, for a formal introduction. At the end of each dance a gentleman was expected to offer his left arm to his partner and lead her to a seat near her chaperone. He would then withdraw as soon as her next partner arrived.

Best dressing

Typical guidelines for late 19th century young ladies recommended gowns 'of a light and gauzy kind, and of a length of skirt that enables the wearer to thread her way without impediment to herself and other dancers'. Trains were considered quite out of place, and an encumbrance even if carried over the arm. For gentlemen the required garb was 'the ordinary black suit that constitutes full evening dress, with very open waistcoat, white necktie, and light lavender or white kid gloves.' A button-hole bouquet of 'choice flowers' was, by this time, considered acceptable.

CORRECT BEHAVIOUR

More rules for balls, as expounded by *Enquire Within*:
- Upon entering, first address the lady of the house; and after her, the nearest acquaintances you may recognize in the room.
- Avoid excess of jewellery.
- Do not select the same partner frequently.
- Never stare about you as if you were taking stock of those present.
- The host and hostess should look after their guests, and not confine their attentions. They should, in fact, attend chiefly to those who are least known in the room.

COUNTRY HOUSE GUESTS ARRIVING BY TRAIN SHOULD BE MET AT THE STATION

MEETING GUESTS WAS TRADITIONALLY THE DUTY OF THE SECOND COACHMAN OR, IN LATER ERAS, THE CHAUFFEUR.

Once guests' arrival had been announced, the hostess would meet and greet them personally. She would, ahead of time, have stipulated whether women guests might be accompanied by their personal maids and men by their valets, chauffeurs and – if shooting was on the agenda – their personal loaders. It was the height of impropriety to arrive with your own staff unless such agreements had been made. It was also polite to arrive at the pre-arranged time.

On arrival at the house, whether by train or by motor car, a man servant took guests' boxes up to their rooms while maids transported ladies' wraps and items such as books and papers. If a lady had not brought her own maid with her, the hostess's own maid took care of a guest's dressing case, including the

AHEAD OF TIME

It was considered good manners to supply guests with details of the train timetable ahead of their arrival and for guests to advise of their plans. As Complete Etiquette for Ladies and Gentlemen **advised:** 'Nothing is more annoying for the host who occupies a remote house than to have to make several long and fruitless journeys to pick up a guest at the station.' **No well-mannered guest ever outstayed their welcome unless, so etiquette manuals stressed** 'invited to do so in a manner that leaves no doubt as to the sincerity of the hostess'.

keys to any luggage, but never those of her jewellery case. It was then the maid's duty to show visitors the locations of the bathroom and where any items removed from boxes had been placed – unpacking being a servant's task.

THE MAID'S ROUTINE

If accompanying her mistress a lady's maid was addressed and referred to by her mistress's surname. During the visit she carried out duties such as these:
- Bringing tea or chocolate as requested.
- Turning on the bath at a specified time.
- Putting out a riding habit, hat and other accoutrements and, if necessary helping her mistress on with her boots.
- Removing for brushing any clothes needing attention during the day.
- In the evening, preparing the bedroom for the night, making sure that hot water was available.
- Lighting a fire and laying out night attire on the bed.

A ROYAL VISIT DEMANDS ETIQUETTE OF THE HIGHEST ORDER

IT WAS IMPERATIVE FOR SUCH A VISIT TO AVOID OFFENCE TO EITHER THE MEMBERS OF THE ROYAL FAMILY OR THE STAFF TRAVELLING WITH THEM.

From the Victorian era onwards, royal guests were most likely to arrive at their venue by train. Local volunteers might form a guard of honour to greet them but, said *The Lady's Realm* of 1904, detailing correct behaviour for a visit from Edward VII and Queen Alexandra, '... no band must be provided or procession arranged'. The King and Queen would then be taken to their venue in a carriage drawn by four horses, with additional carriages being provided for royal staff and for luggage. On arrival, says the piece: 'The hostess will meet her Royal guests at the entrance to the castle or mansion in the usual way.'

HOUSE PARTY ETIQUETTE

Should a house party be involved – but only if this was the stated wish of the royal guests – then it was left to the host and hostess to draw up the invitation list, relying as *The Lady's Realm* of 1904 says *'on their good taste in the matter'* with the caveat that they '*... may not be conversant with some little matter which may have come to the ears of the King's entourage, and so an undesirable may occasionally be included.'*

A ROYAL DINNER

The timetable for a stately country house dinner with King Edward VII and Queen Alexandra early in the 20th century ran as follows:

8.55: All guests assemble in the saloon or drawing-room and form up in an avenue with ladies on one side and gentlemen on the other.

9.00: King and Queen arrive. His Majesty leads in the hostess, the host, the Queen. They walk through the avenue of bowing guests, who then follow in order of precedence, with gentlemen offering their right arms to ladies.

9.15: Dinner is served with the King and Queen being waited on by their own servants, receiving dishes brought to them by servants of the household.

10.00 or thereabouts: The King exits the dining-room. The ladies go to the drawing-room. Gentlemen follow the King to the smoking-rooms.

10.30: The King and gentlemen join the ladies, at which point additional guests may have arrived to be presented to the royal couple. Entertainment may then follow such as private theatricals.

Schedule for the day

Next morning, breakfast was served to the royal guests in their own apartments and, unless it was the shooting season, they might stay in their rooms for most of the morning. Luncheon would be taken with any other guests. When, in the Edwardian era, many small tables were laid for this meal, host and hostess sat with their Majesties, 'with others of the company being honoured by invitations in turn.' Whatever the activities of the afternoon – anything from strolling in the grounds to the planting of memorial trees – the whole party would meet for an informal afternoon tea which was 'always the occasion for a pleasant exchange of courtesies and cheerful conversation.'

Freedom to roam

During the day, royal visitors had the freedom to visit any part of the house or garden as they wished. When Princess Victoria stayed at Chatsworth in 1832, aged 13, for her first dinner party she inspected the kitchen and pronounced it 'superb' both in dimensions and cleanliness. To keep the gardens perfect for her visit, head gardener Joseph Paxton (1803–65, designer of the Crystal Palace), employed the services of around 100 men to remove any fallen leaves and branches and to keep the paths clear and all the lawns perfectly rolled.

TIPPING IS A SERIOUS ITEM IN THE EXPENSES OF COUNTRY HOUSE VISITS

HOUSE STAFF MIGHT WELL EXPECT TO RECEIVE TIPS FROM GUESTS, BUT IT WAS ALWAYS WISE TO CHECK AHEAD WITH THE HOST WHO MIGHT DISAPPROVE OR EXPRESSLY FORBID IT.

The practice of tipping began in coffee houses and taverns in 18th-century England and signs 'to insure promptitude' were prominently displayed to encourage patrons to tip and so hasten service. In the same period it also became accepted that country house guests would tip the servants of their hosts; the money given to the servants was known as 'vails'.

Lining up for rewards

It was customary, when a guest was leaving the house, for the servants to line up in a double rank outside the door and for the guest to proffer a vail to each in turn. This could certainly be expensive. A German nobleman, Baron de Pollnitz, having visited an English stately home said bitterly that '...if a Duke gives me Dinner four Times a Week, his Footmen would pocket as much of my Money as would serve my Expenses at the Tavern for a Week.'

In houses where tipping was forbidden the good mistress recompensed her staff with special monetary arrangements depending on the number and status of the guests entertained. If she failed to do this, staff would feel extremely ill used.

TIPPING PRACTICE

During the 19th century, tipping became more random but in the Edwardian era tipping once again became formalized and also more generous, the amount given depending, so 'Madge' (Mrs Humphry) writing in *Every Woman's Encyclopedia* in 1910 said, *'on the circumstances and particularly on the position and social standing of the visitor'.* She also described a practice carried out in a few country houses: *'On the day when a guest terminates a visit the menservants are allowed to throw themselves in his or her way and they have to be tipped.'*

'Madge' advised these amounts for tipping. In addition tips would be given to servants who cleaned boots. Tips for bedroom servants would be left in the bedroom. (A half crown was 2 shillings and 6 pence, which is 12½ pence in today's money.):

- **Butler**: a sovereign for a few days' visit.
- **Chauffeur**: from half a sovereign upwards if there have been many motor car rides, but if he only meets guests at the station and returns them there, five shillings or three half crowns.
- **Maid**: five shillings to the maid who looks after a woman visitor's room.
- **Footman**: half a crown for carrying luggage.
- **Parlour maid**: also half a crown for luggage carrying.

THE ARRANGEMENT OF THE HAIR IS MOST IMPORTANT

THE HAIR, AND THE MODE IN WHICH IT WAS ARRANGED AT DIFFERENT TIMES OF DAY, WAS SOCIALLY SIGNIFICANT.

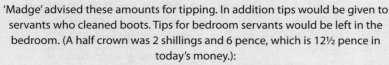

Tending to the hair was the task of the lady's maid. Until the 1920s, no lady of standing would have short hair and it would always be topped with a hat. Equally hair was never worn 'down' in public, although young girls might have lower parts of the coiffeur hanging in ringlets. By the Edwardian era styles had become incredibly elaborate, with slightly looser styles being preferred for daytime wear than at night or on formal

occasions when a tiara was worn.

The daily routine

Before her mistress retired for bed the lady's maid unpinned and brushed her hair then plaited it. Before styling it the following morning it was brushed again. For elaborate styles the hair was rolled over frizettes, fabricated from hair and chosen to match the hair colour of the wearer, but which needed to remain totally hidden. Since the hair was washed infrequently pomades were used to add shine. A typical mixture comprised castor oil and melted white wax scented with bergamot oil or oil of lavender. To equip her for the arts of hairdressing a would-be lady's maid might be tutored by a professional practitioner.

ADVICE FOR HAIR DRESSING

Mrs Beeton said that: *'If ringlets are worn, remove the curl-papers, and, after thoroughly brushing the back hair both above and below, dress it according to the prevailing fashion. If bandeaux are worn, the hair is thoroughly brushed and frizzed outside and inside....'*

DECORATIONS AND DIAMONDS
If a tiara was not worn, for a formal country house dinner, a woman might instruct her maid to weave ribbons or lace into her hair or add a feather decoration or even artificial flowers or fruit. With a tiara, long hair was always worn 'up'.

THE HOSTESS IS AN OSTENSIBLE CHAPERONE AT PARTIES TO WHICH GIRLS ARE ASKED WITH THEIR MOTHERS

IF HER MOTHER WAS OTHERWISE ENGAGED, IT WAS THE HOSTESS'S DUTY TO MAKE SURE THAT A GIRL WAS PROTECTED FROM THE UNDUE ATTENTIONS OF MEN REGARDED AS UNSUITABLE.

During country house visits there were various occasions on which young women could escape from close scrutiny, for even the best chaperone could not possibly supervise her charge 24 hours a day. Outdoor activities such as tennis and hunting provided good opportunities for mixing with men whom chaperones might consider unsuitable – roués, upstarts, married men and those deemed to have limited prospects in the marriage market.

BREAKING THE RULES

For the extremely daring there was scope at night for 'bedroom hopping', which might even be aided by the hostess, as Vita (also known as Victoria) Sackville-West described in her 1930 novel *The Edwardians*: 'The name of each guest would be neatly written on a card slipped into a tiny brass frame on the bedroom door. This question of the disposition of bedrooms always gave the duchess and her fellow-hostesses cause for anxious thought. It was so necessary to be tactful, and at the same time discreet. The professional Lothario would be furious if he found himself in a room surrounded by ladies who were all accompanied by their husbands.'

Making good matches

Chaperones aside, country house parties were instrumental in the marriage market, coming as they did after the London Season (or for the less wealthy and well connected a series of summer balls and dinners) at which great efforts were made for eligible young men and women to meet. Hostesses with an eye for matchmaking would draw up their guest lists with this in view, particularly if they were mothers to sons and heirs who had not yet found suitable brides.

Snobbery was relevant too, since some ambitious mothers regarded any man but the heir to an estate as totally unacceptable. And many young girls brought up in the country were likely to have a limited life experience and little self confidence, making them easily dazzled by men with polish and charm.

THERE ARE MANY TALKERS BUT FEW WHO KNOW HOW TO CONVERSE AGREEABLY

KNOWING HOW TO MAKE GOOD CONVERSATION WAS AN OBLIGATORY ACCOMPLISHMENT FOR ANY COUNTRY HOUSE GUEST, AND A MEASURE OF GOOD BREEDING WITHIN THE FAMILY ALSO.

For both men and women the advice was to speak distinctly, and neither too fast or too slowly. However there were specific rules pertinent to each sex.

For women ...

Women wishing their conversation to be agreeable were given strict instructions from manuals of the day to 'avoid

BREAKING THE CODE

Exceptions to the rules might apply to young men of high birth, as *Society Small Talk* **of 1879 explained:** *'The broad and airy compliments of which men of a certain standing consider themselves privileged to pay to young ladies are not to be paid indiscriminately by ordinary mortals, the right of doing so belonging to those men who have a recognised reputation for this style of persiflage [banter].'*

conceit or affectation, and laughter which is not natural and spontaneous'. Moreover, their language needed to be 'easy and unstudied, marked by a graceful carelessness, which, at the same time, never oversteps the limits of propriety. Her lips' she was reminded, 'will readily yield to a pleasant smile; she will not love to hear herself talk; her tones will bear the impress of sincerity, and her eye kindle with animation as she speaks.' And there were strict warnings against interrupting, considered as extremely rude, and of 'pushing, to its full extent, a discussion which has become unpleasant'.

KNOWING THE ESSENTIALS
Advice on conversation included:
- Accommodate the pitch of your voice to the hearing of the person with whom you are conversing.
- Never speak with your mouth full.
- Laugh only after telling jokes, not before or during their relation.
- Always avoid the topics of politics and religion.
- For both sexes a ball is an occasion on which small talk is totally acceptable.

... and for men

For men, it was unacceptable to show off with quotes in Greek or Latin or to indulge in pedantry. Equally men were counselled: 'If you feel intellectual superiority to any one with whom you are conversing, do not seek to bear him down; it would be an inglorious triumph, and a breach of good manners.' However skilled their conversation it was always unacceptable for house party guests to form themselves into 'sets', such behaviour being 'an affront to their host'.

WHENEVER LONG GLOVES ARE WORN THEY SHOULD BE KEPT ON UNTIL ALL THE GUESTS ARE SEATED AT TABLE, WHEN THEY MAY BE REMOVED

FOR WOMEN, LONG GLOVES WERE ESSENTIAL FOR FORMAL COUNTRY HOUSE DINNER PARTIES, BUT REQUIRED CAREFUL TREATMENT.

With full-length evening dress, long gloves were *de rigeur* for women and, whether they had buttons or not, were traditionally measured in terms of 'buttons' (one button is approximately an inch or 25 mm). An elbow length glove is a 16-button, a mid-bicep glove a 22-button and a shoulder length glove a 30-button. Good manners demanded that the only jewellery worn over a glove of any length should be bracelets – never rings.

Successful removal

To remove gloves they needed to be carefully folded down to the wrist before being delicately pulled from the tips of the fingers and thumb to avoid turning them inside out. On no account should the teeth ever be involved in their removal. Finally, they were expected to be laid across the lap and under a table napkin. After dinner, ladies replaced their gloves for dancing, but kept them removed for playing cards.

COURSES AT DINNER SHOULD BE CONSUMED IN THE CORRECT ORDER

THE RULE FOR DINING IN AN AGE WHEN PEOPLE HELPED THEMSELVES TO FOOD SERVED *À LA FRANÇAISE*, OR FROM A BUFFET LAID OUT FOR A BALL OR WEDDING BREAKFAST.

Until the style of dining changed to service *à la Russe* in the 19th century, with each course being served separately, food for a formal dinner, (sometimes including desserts), was placed on the table at the start of the meal, along with candles and other ornaments, plus flowers, pyramids of fruit and salt in fancy containers. The table was stylishly set out symmetrically, with many dishes placed in pairs. Polite guests would serve themselves from the dishes placed nearest to them and, if necessary, pass dishes to their neighbours and help them with carving and cutting as necessary.

The pattern of dinner

Dinner took a set pattern. First to be eaten was the soup, in two or more varieties, ladelled from large tureens. Following  these were the 'removes', dishes such as fish, cutlets and tongue, plus roast turkey, mutton or chicken. Eaten with these were *hors d'ouevres* (literally outside the main dish) placed around the table, which might include dishes such as small pies, oysters, eggs, and radishes.

When all these had been cleared away, the second course or *entremets* was eaten, consisting of large roasts accompanied by both vegetables and sweet dishes – creams, jellies and ices. The tablecloth might then be removed and either replaced with a clean one or the final course of dessert cheese, pastries, sweet concoctions and fruit replaced direct onto the table.

DINNER IN VERSE

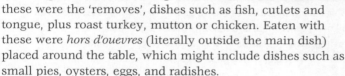

Amazed at the array of dishes set before him at a dinner party held by Lord and Lady Amundeville in his satiric early 19th century poem 'Don Juan', Byron penned the lines:

Their table was a board to tempt even ghosts
To pass the Styx for more substantial feasts.
I will not dwell upon ragoûts or roasts,
Albeit all human history attests
That happiness for man – the hungry sinner! –
Since Eve ate apples, much depends on dinner.

For a ball supper or wedding breakfast, all the food was laid on a table or sideboard, with large joints carved on the sideboard or in the kitchen ahead of serving. In 1861 Mrs Beeton in her bill of fare for a winter ball supper for 60 included more than 30 different dishes including:

• Lobster salad; prawns.

• Tongue, ornamented, boiled fowls with béchamel sauce; boar's head garnished with aspic jelly; mayonnaise of fowl; galantine of veal; roast pheasant; small ham, garnished; larded capon, raised game pie.

• Swiss cream; meringues, custards in glasses; fruited jelly, vanilla cream; biscuits and raspberry cream.

FOOD IS SERVED FROM THE LEFT, WINE FROM THE RIGHT

THE UNBREAKABLE RULE FOR SERVICE AT TABLE WHEN EACH COURSE IS SERVED SEPARATELY.

TO ACCOMPANY DESSERT

While dessert was being handed to guests the butler follows, says *The Servants' Practical Guide* '... with the claret and sherry of which he offers the choice. When he has made the round of the table, he places two full decanters of sherry and a claret jug of claret before the master of the house, and thus, having completed the duty of waiting at table, he leaves the dining-room, followed by the other servants.'

Compared with dining *à la Française*, the 'new' 19th-century *à la Russe* style of service demanded many servants to be on hand to bring in the dishes for each course. The rule was that food would either be offered from a large dish from which diners could help themselves or be served by the footman. Ladies seated on the right and left hand of the host were served first, followed by each guest in succession. If there was a choice of dishes, then the footman asked the diner which was preferred.

Silently correct

Noiseless service, apart from necessary questions to diners, was obligatory for servants. No clatter of any kind was acceptable. Servants were expected to move quietly, briskly and silently around the table. Serving drinks was the butler's duty, with guests offered choices as appropriate. At a Victorian dinner hock or Chablis was served with oysters, sherry with soup and champagne, opened on the sideboard, with the fish and meat. Claret would also be offered 'throughout dinner in lieu of any other wine'.

SPECIAL SHELLFISH

Oysters were an exception to the rules of service, as *The Servants' Practical Guide* says: *'To hand a large dish of oysters reposing on a serviette to each guest in succession is worse than bad style; it is awkward and inconvenient for the guests to help themselves from the dish.'* Instead, they were placed in position before guests entered the dining room.

FOLLOWING DINNER, THE LADIES SHOULD WITHDRAW TO THE DRAWING ROOM

HERE THEY WERE SERVED TEA, COFFEE AND POSSIBLY LIQUEURS, LEAVING THE MEN TO ENJOY THEMSELVES IN THE DINING ROOM OR A SMOKING ROOM.

It was essential for ladies to read the signs and to know when to make a move, since the signal to leave might be a subtle nod or smile to the senior female guest – the one who had been escorted to dinner by the host. The hostess was instructed to time the exit carefully, avoiding the moment when a guest had just laid down their knife, fork, or glass. Equally, it was polite to let an animated or interesting conversation follow its course

TOPICS OF CONVERSATION

Conversation among the ladies would undoubtedly have been light and even gossipy. This might not be to everyone's taste, as Jane Austen, complaining of the *'poverty of conversation'* noted in *Sense and Sensibility* '... *the gentlemen had supplied the discourse with some variety – the variety of politics, inclosing land and breaking horses – but then it was all over, and one subject only engaged the ladies till coffee came in, which was the comparative heights of Harry Dashwood and Lady Middleton's son William, who were nearly of the same age.'*

before leaving. If, on the other hand, the mood of the dinner was marred by disagreement or an unwelcome topic then a speedy withdrawal could be to everyone's advantage.

IN THE CORRECT ORDER

To concur with the rules of etiquette, ladies left the dining room in the same order as they had entered it, that is according to rank and age, and with married women – including widows – taking precedence over the single.

IT IS ESSENTIAL THAT THE PORT IS PASSED CORRECTLY AND THAT CIGARS ARE WELL STORED

THE PERFECT COUNTRY HOUSE HOST STILL ENSURES THAT EVERYTHING SERVED AFTER DINNER IS OF THE HIGHEST QUALITY.

Vintage port was decanted by the butler before dinner to free it of both crust and sediment. First to take the port decanter is the host, who pours a glass for the guest on his right. He then passes the decanter to the left. Each person fills his own glass, then hands the decanter to the next

---

TOPICS OF CONVERSATION

Over port and cigars men would continue in political and possibly ribald conversation. But while in the early 19th century they might be summoned by a butler to join the ladies for coffee, by the 1920s they were expected to be polite enough to bring an end to their own gathering and adjourn in good time.

person to the left. When the decanter reaches the host he pours himself a glass. As the decanter is passed it should never touch the table or be lifted over a glass.

Cigars made of choice tobacco would be proffered to every male guest, and the host (and butler) made sure that they were stored in an airtight cedar wood box kept at an even temperature. The polite guest trusted his host to provide cigars of the highest quality. It was the height of bad manners to test the dryness of the leaf by putting it to his ear and rolling it in his fingers.

THE ETIQUETTE OF CIGARS

Whoever was serving at table – either butler or footman – needed to make sure that a cigar cutter was to hand for removing the 'cap' before it could be smoked and for offering a taper to light it. What was most important was for the cigar to be evenly lit all around so that it did not burn raggedly. Removing the band from the cigar was acceptable as long as this was done a few minutes after the cigar was lit and was taken off without tearing.

THE BUSINESS OF THE HOUSE SHOULD NEVER BE DISCUSSED WITH STRANGERS

JUST ONE OF MANY RULES FOR COUNTRY HOUSE STAFF REGARDING CONVERSATION. SERVANTS WERE ALWAYS EXPECTED TO BE AS UNOBTRUSIVE AS POSSIBLE.

Discretion was of paramount importance in the country house. It was obligatory that family matters, which staff might well overhear, were not broadcast to visitors, including the servants of house guests, let alone to any visiting trades people or casual labourers. It was unacceptable for staff even to indicate, by some facial expression, that they had heard the conversation of a family member or guest, or have been aware of talk at the dinner table. Doubtless such matters were discussed in the kitchen or servants' hall – at least beyond the hearing of senior staff.

A good career

Employment in a country house was considered, for a country boy or young man, a worthwhile lifetime career and most country house staff were much more contented than their city counterparts, not least because landowners made efforts to make them feel part of a worthwhile community.

RULES FOR SERVANTS

In 1901 the Ladies' Sanitary Association published *Rules for the Manners of Servants in Good Families,* **many of which applied to the spoken word, among them were:**

'Nosiness is considered bad manners.'

'Always move quietly about the house, and do not let your voice be heard by the family unless necessary. Never sing or whistle at your work where the family would be likely to hear you.'

'Do not call out from one room to another; and if you are a housemaid, be careful not only to do your work quietly, but to keep out of sight as much as possible.'

'Never begin to talk to the ladies or gentlemen, unless it be to deliver a message or ask a necessary question, and then do it in as few words as possible.'

'Do not talk to your fellow servants, or to the children of the family in passages or sitting rooms, or in the presence of ladies and gentlemen, unless necessary, and then speak to them very quietly.'

'Always speak of the children of the family as "Master", "Miss".'

THERE IS AN ORDER OF PRECEDENCE IN THE SERVANTS' HALL

EVEN BELOW STAIRS THERE WAS A STRICT HIERARCHY AMONG THE STAFF, PARTICULARLY AT MEALTIMES.

Below stairs, the senior servants or 'pugs' set the rules for correct behaviour. In large country houses with many staff, the most senior members, known as the 'Upper Ten' were privileged to have their own dining room, or 'Pug's Parlour', which might be the room of the housekeeper or the house steward. Often the 'pugs' dined here for an entire meal, being waited on by the steward's footman. If senior staff joined their junior colleagues for dinner, the ritual was that the 'pugs' entered the servants' hall for the first part of the meal, arriving in formal array, and in order of precedence, while the lower staff stood in deference.

All then took their seats at the long table, with the housekeeper at the head. To her right would sit the cook, to her left the lady's maid. On each side of the table women staff sat by rank, creating an all-female congregation. The opposite end of the table was headed by the steward or butler with the under-butler to his right and the coachman to his left. As with women staff, the men sat by rank, in descending order, so that men and women – in reality most probably boys and girls – of lowest rank were placed in the middle.

MEALTIME DUTIES
To begin the meal, grace was said by the most senior person, then the meat course was served. Any carving needed was the butler's duty. The 'pugs' then retired to their own dining room, taking with them the necessary china and glass to consume dessert and cheese, washed down with claret or another wine. On their way out of the hall they might express their disdain at drinking the beer provided by tipping any that remained in their glasses into the sink on their way out – a ritual dubbed 'sinking the beer'.

ENTERTAINMENT, LEISURE AND SPORT

The country house was – and remains – the perfect place for relaxation and sport, from hunting, shooting and fishing to tennis, croquet and leisurely strolls around the grounds. It was also ideal for entertaining not only friends but those people the master and mistress of the house wished to court for social, political or commercial reasons, from the captains of industry to royalty. Indoor pursuits were an essential part of a country house visit, and could include cards, charades and musical entertainment. And within the confines of a country house, gambling games that were illegal in other settings were played without compunction.

Informal relaxation

Many of the sporting activities of the country house provided opportunities for men and women to mix freely in a way that was impossible in more formal circumstances and the country house party was an accepted way for eligible and 'suitable' bachelors to be introduced to girls considered to be in need of good husbands. When such a match was made, the country house was the ideal location for a lavish wedding reception.

Time off

For country house servants, leisure time was minimal and much appreciated when it became available. Since most of the junior staff were recruited locally, days off were an opportunity for them to visit their families or to make excursions to local shops and hostelries. In most houses it was also possible for visitors to be entertained in the servants' quarters, as long as no improprieties took place. Traditionally, Twelfth Night was the date for the annual servants' ball, with family and staff reversing roles for the night and mingling on the dance floor.

THERE IS AN ABIDING CHARM TO A GARDEN PARTY

TEA IN THE GARDEN BECAME COMMON COUNTRY HOUSE
PRACTICE IN THE VICTORIAN ERA. DRESS, EXCEPT FOR
THOSE EXERTING THEMSELVES IN SPORT WAS, HOWEVER,
DECIDEDLY FORMAL.

Typical advice to garden party hostesses was that the
event should be synchronized with a display of roses
or some other favoured flower and, given the vagaries of
the British climate, that indoor rooms should be prepared
in case of rain. Guests were invited to arrive at 3.30 or 4.00
and greeted by their hostess in a shady spot before tea was
served in bone china cups at small tables set with good
linen. The hour for departure would be 7 o'clock after guests
had played games such as tennis and croquet if they so
wished and, at a grand party, been entertained by a band
playing popular music.

For the Victorian garden party, dress was as formal as for
an indoor tea party but daintier. Women wore long dresses
of silk or chiffon (pale colours were acceptable for all except
those in mourning), plus hats and gloves. Parasols were
carried to protect complexions from the sun, it being
considered indelicate to allow the skin to tan.

Men were expected to don suits or military uniforms,
as appropriate. Similar rules pertained in the Edwardian era
and it was only in the 1920s that fashion changed radically
in favour of looser dresses,

CUCUMBER CRITICIZED

**As a sandwich filling, cucumber was
considered cold and undesirable, as the
last verse of a poem published in the
magazine *Punch* describes:**
So much for cold John Cucumber,
Whom few insides can stand,
Of all the Cucurbitae
The worst in Merrie England.

often bias cut and with chiffon overlays that created a floating, fluttering effect. Floral dresses only became the vogue in the 1950s, but hats were still worn for formal garden parties.

Garden party sandwiches

The sandwich, made using white bread and with the crusts removed, became a garden party staple, and until the mid 19th century when cucumber became popular, would have been of ham tongue or beef. Gentleman's Relish or Patum Peperium, an anchovy paste invented in 1828 by John Osborn and made to a recipe still carefully guarded, was another popular sandwich filling.

HOME GROWN AND MADE

As well as sandwiches and cakes, and strawberries and cream (using home grown fruit from the kitchen garden), jellies, and ices were popular foods for summer country house garden parties, all served by the house staff under the direction of the butler. Making ices was possible thanks to the ice houses constructed in the grounds and kept filled all year round.

CROQUET MAY BE PLAYED BY PERSONS OF ALL AGES AND OF EITHER SEX

BY THE 1860S CROQUET WAS THE NUMBER ONE OUTDOOR SOCIAL PASTIME; EVERY BIG HOUSE WOULD HAVE A SET OF BALLS, MALLETS AND HOOPS TO SET OUT ON THE LAWN.

Croquet was regarded as a 'delightful and health-giving sport' and perfectly suitable for young Victorian ladies. One of the earliest croquet lawns was at Cassiobury Park in Hertfordshire, owned by Arthur Algernon Capel, sixth Earl of Essex. The Earl, a leading entertainer in high society who quickly caught the 'croquet bug', not only hosted lavish croquet parties but marketed the Cassiobury brand croquet set, manufactured in his own sawmills.

Unlike tennis, croquet could be played in ordinary outdoor dress – tweeds being suitable for men or a blazer and boater.

FOUL PLAY

Among its many instructions for players *Enquire Within* of 1894 included the following in its list of 'foul strokes':
- To spoon, that is, to push the ball without an audible knock.
- To strike a ball twice in the same stroke.
- To stop a ball with the foot in taking a loose Croquet.
- To allow a ball to touch the mallet in rebounding from the turning peg.
- If a player, in striking at a ball which lies against a peg or wire, should move it from position by striking a peg or wire, the ball must be replaced, and the stroke taken again.

It was thus perfect garden party entertainment and a chance for unmarried men and women to meet free from the close scrutiny of a chaperone.

IT IS FASHIONABLE FOR THE ARISTOCRACY TO ADD TENNIS COURTS TO THEIR COUNTRY HOUSES

OR SO IT WAS IN THE VICTORIAN AND EDWARDIAN ERAS, WHEN LAWN TENNIS BECAME POPULAR FOR BOTH MEN AND WOMEN.

Tennis was greatly helped by the invention of the lawnmower in 1830, which allowed grass to be cut short. Frequent rolling, done by one of the groundsmen, was also necessary to keep the court smooth. Typical of its time was the tennis court created at Hatfield House in 1842 by the second Marquis of Salisbury. He played his first game there against the Revd F.G. Faithfull, who was then Rector of Hatfield. The lawn was marked out with white chalk, although in some places tapes were pinned to the ground for the purpose. Now part of a private club, the court is still played on today.

ROYAL APPROVAL

In 1845, Queen Victoria was a spectator at a game of tennis at Stratfield Saye, home of the Duke of Wellington on the Hampshire/ Berkshire border. In her diary she recorded *'... a very fine game played between Ld. Charles, the Duke's marker, & a fat man called Philips, the Duke's butler, who plays beautifully.'*

What to wear

The good hostess not only provided enough racquets for everyone but ensured that her guests were well informed about dress. Until 1910 women wore hats, tight-sleeved jackets and heavy skirts with tight waists while men donned full-length white trousers and long sleeved shirts. Rubber-soled shoes, introduced in 1867, were *de rigueur* for serious players. More amateur performers wore boots or substantial shoes of some kind.

GOOD MANNERS

On court it was deemed impolite to make audible comments disparaging others' play or to lose one's temper. At the end of a match, shaking hands and thanking one's partner and opponents were also essential. A substantial but informal tennis tea, as for a garden party (see There is an abiding charm to a garden party), was served outside on good china.

THERE ARE FEW MORE DELIGHTFUL ENTERTAINMENTS THAN A CRICKET MATCH

ALTHOUGH IT BEGAN AS A WORKING MAN'S GAME, CRICKET SOON BECAME POPULAR IN THE PERFECT SETTING OF THE COUNTRY HOUSE.

Some of the earliest country house cricket matches were held in the mid 18th century at Knole in Kent, home of the 1st Duke of Dorset. The Knole pitch was maintained in prime condition by Valentine Romney, a prime player of his day. Pavilions were also added, like the exceptional example at Hemingford Park in Cambridgeshire, where matches even took place against county sides. Here gentlemen (i.e. amateur) players, including such great names as W.G. Grace and C.B. Fry, stayed as guests in the main house while any professionals were accommodated in one of the three bedrooms on the first floor of the pavilion.

A cricket match was a social occasion – often the focus of a country house weekend – and a chance for men and women to parade in their finery. Beyond sporting prowess, gambling was also the order of the day, with stakes ranging up to great heights, such as the 200 guineas won in 1800 by Squire Osbaleston from Lord George Bentinck.

GREAT ENTERTAINMENT

Between innings, country house cricketers might be entertained to a large lunch. Lord William Lennox, writing in the 1870s sets the scene: *'A party sallied forth from the house headed by my father… They had quitted the dining-room after imbibing a fair quantity of port wine, leaving instructions to the butler that clean glasses, devilled biscuits, and a magnum of "beeswing" [a well aged port complete with crust] should be ready on their return from the cricket field.'*

FISHING IS AN EXCELLENT SPORT FOR GUESTS

FROM THE COUNTRY HOUSE, FISHING COULD TAKE PLACE FROM A LAKE, RIVER OR STREAM. FISHING FROM A BOAT WAS PARTICULARLY PLEASURABLE.

An exceptional room

At Kedleston Hall in Derbyshire the magnificent fishing room on two floors, designed by Robert Adam was ornamented with stone carvings, still life paintings of fish and seascapes. From a Venetian window on the upper storey women could fish in comfort away from the sun (lest their complexions suffer). Below, in the basement, were two boathouses and a plunge bath.

At the grandest houses, freshwater fishing expeditions began and ended at a pavilion or room on the lake in the grounds, from which boats could be launched and where the catch could be cooked and eaten immediately. This kind of fishing was an acceptable entertainment for women as well as men.

Good country house hosts kept their waters well stocked with fish and supplied rods for guests – and possibly fishing gear such as waders as well, since fly fishing for salmon and trout often involved walking into the water chest high. In the winter months, anglers rubbed their legs with goose fat to protect themselves from the cold. Whisky was kept to hand for warming fishermen as they retreated regularly from midstream to the bank.

IN PRAISE OF FISHING

At Antony House in Cornwall in 1610 the translator and antiquary Richard Carew (1555–1620) composed this poem in praise of his fishpond, which also tells of the species it contained:

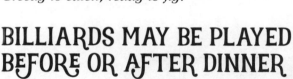

My fishful pond is my delight
There sucking mullet, swallowing bass,
Side-walking crabs, wry-mouthed fluke,
And slip-first eel, as evenings pass,
For safe bait at due place do look,
Bold to approach, quick to espy,
Greedy to catch, ready to fly.

BILLIARDS MAY BE PLAYED BEFORE OR AFTER DINNER

POPULAR ALL YEAR ROUND AS A COUNTRY HOUSE ENTERTAINMENT, BILLIARDS BEGAN AS A GAME FOR BOTH SEXES.

In country houses the hall often served as a billiard room, being the only space large enough to accommodate the large table with its massive legs. But from the 18th century, as the game became increasingly popular, the table was often afforded its own space, ideally lit from above.

Although women enjoyed billiards, in houses where the billiard room

Family fun

Among families, a fast and furious game called billiard fives developed, as described by Deborah, the Duchess of Devonshire, in her memoirs. In this, the prime objective was to hit the ball down the table fast enough so by the time it returned, the person running behind you had no hope of hitting it, thereby losing a point.

doubled as a smoking room it was largely a male preserve. As well as following the basic rule of stooping so as to get eyes, ball and object ball in a straight line, it was essential to take care never to commit the cardinal sin of mis-cueing and ripping the green baize (felt) covering the table. It was also bad manners to stand close to a player or to make a noise, such as lighting a match, whilst they were making a shot. Early evening billiards was always halted by the bell warning guests to retire to their rooms to change for dinner.

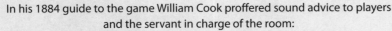

CARE OF THE BILLIARD ROOM

In his 1884 guide to the game William Cook proffered sound advice to players and the servant in charge of the room:

- Cues should always be kept in an upright position and replaced in the rack immediately after play.
- Always brush the cloth every time the table has been played on, brushing with the nap and pushing dirt into the pockets.
- Iron the cloth regularly.
- Avoid letting the room get too cold. If necessary warm the cushions with tin boxes filled with hot water designed specifically for this purpose.

A SHOOTING PARTY REQUIRES A SUSTAINING LUNCHEON

AND MORE BESIDES. A DAY'S SHOOTING WAS HARD WORK FOR STAFF NEEDING TO ENSURE AN EXCELLENT DAY FOR ALL CONCERNED.

In the kitchen, a shooting day might begin as early as 4.30 in the morning, when staff would prepare sandwiches for the beaters. They would also begin making an elaborate luncheon for the 'guns', their lady companions and the gun loaders, which needed to be transported to an outdoor spot along with trestle tables and chairs, tablecloths and other linens, plus glasses and cutlery. If the weather was inclement, arrangements were made for the meal to be served in the gamekeeper's cottage.

Since a shoot normally lasted three days (traditionally Tuesday to Thursday) variety was also essential.

A sport for princes

While previous generations shot largely to keep down vermin and to kill game, shooting on country house estates became high sport after the Prince of Wales (the future Edward VII) purchased the Sandringham estate in Norfolk in 1862. Here literally thousands of birds, rabbits and hares were shot each year according to a strict calendar.

STAFF DUTIES

A pony and gig was needed to ferry the luncheon to the shooting party. Hot food was piled into sacks or put into pans, which were then inserted into wooden 'hot boxes' insulated with padding.

After each day's shooting staff were required to count and hang birds in game larders and pluck any that were to be eaten for dinner that night before cleaning muddy boots and brushing down clothes.

Popular hot luncheon dishes included stews, casseroles, curries, suet puddings and roast meats accompanied by baked potatoes; typical cold fare included game pie, ham and other meats. Apple dumplings or turnovers, rice pudding and rib-sticking steamed puddings such as spotted dick made ideal desserts on winter days.

... and to drink

The butler and footmen – who always served the meal – would proffer wine, beer or cider. While guests were enjoying their feast, the loaders dined on jacket potatoes and meat while the beaters had bread and cheese.

HUNTING IS BOTH A SPORT AND A SOCIAL OCCASION

BY EDWARDIAN TIMES BOTH MEN AND WOMEN COULD PARTICIPATE MORE OR LESS EQUALLY IN THE FIELD, IF NOT IN THE CELEBRATORY ASPECTS OF THE DAY.

From November 1st, the start of the fox hunting season, the men of the household would eat a cooked breakfast before venturing out into the field. Ahead of the hunt, vintage port was served indoors to male members of the family and any hunt dignitaries while outside the house, the butler and footmen served a lesser variety of port to the men. Later in the morning the whole party returned for a hunt breakfast 'proper' in the dining room, to be served – again to the men only – by the butler and to include wine, beer and spirits. The women who had been hunting breakfasted more soberly in the drawing room with the mistress of the house.

Evening entertainment

Later in the day celebration was paramount. Lord Hervey, guest of the 18th-century Parliamentarian Horace Walpole described the evening celebrations as 'noisy, jolly, drunk, comical and pure merry... We used to sit down to dinner a little snug party of about thirty odd, up to the chin in beef, venison, geese, turkeys, etc; and generally over the chin in claret, strong beer and punch.'

FREEDOM IN THE SADDLE

Women took great pleasure in the freedom of riding in the countryside and leaping hedges, gates and brooks. But it could be dangerous, as Anthony Trollope describes in his 1872 essay *Hunting the Fox: 'To Lizzie it seemed as though the river were the blackest, and the deepest, and the broadest that ever ran. For a moment her heart quailed – but it was but for a moment. She shut her eyes, and gave the little horse his head. For a moment she thought she was in the water... But she was light and the beast made good his footing and she knew she had done it.'*

FEMALE ACCOMPLISHMENTS
Riding to hounds demanded particular skill from women who were obliged to ride side-saddle, dressed in long skirts. But because they were not chaperoned, they had the opportunity to talk openly with their male companions.

AFTER DINNER, CHARADES MAY BE ACTED IN COSTUMES

CHARADES CAME TO THE COUNTRY HOUSE FROM THE COURTS OF EUROPE AND WERE ORIGINALLY RIDDLES ACTED OUT AS DRAMAS TO BE SOLVED BY THE ASSEMBLED COMPANY.

The charades of 19th-century Britain were elaborate affairs and family members not only rehearsed their sketches but dressed up in costumes to mime a word or phrase that had to be guessed. Plenty of props would be used, too. Contemporary books such as *Household Amusements and Family Recreation*, published by Samuel Beeton, husband of the famous cookery writer, supplied texts, sometimes amounting to short plays, for actors to learn or recite.

Other types of charades took the form of conundrums. In every case, each syllable of the word to be guessed was designated 'my first', 'my second', and so on to 'the whole'.

ACTING IT OUT

Advising on charades, *Enquire Within* says: *'Charades may be sentimental or humorous, in poetry or prose; they may also be acted, in which manner they afford considerable amusement.* To do this to best effect it suggested using a variety of household appliances *'employed to fit up something like and stage'* and that *'Characters dressed in costumes made up of handkerchiefs, coats, shawls, table-covers &c, come on and perform an extempore play ….'*

FOR LARGE PARTIES, THERE SHOULD BE A TABLE FOR CARDS, AND TWO PACKS OF CARDS PLACED UPON EACH TABLE

PLAYING CARDS WAS A POPULAR AFTER DINNER ACTIVITY AT THE COUNTRY HOUSE, WITH GAMBLING ALLOWED IN SOME ESTABLISHMENTS.

Following dinner a whole variety of card games were played, of which whist, a game for four people, was the most popular in the 1880s. Also enjoyed were loo, best with five or seven players, and vingt-un for two or more. Bézique, played with two packs of cards with the twos, threes, fours, fives and sixes removed, was another absorbing after dinner game.

A SCANDALOUS GAME

As a result of a royal scandal, baccarat was discontinued in polite society, but almost simultaneously bridge was introduced and became an overnight craze with women in particular.

Bridge was so popular that *The Lady's Realm* even ran an article entitled 'Is Bridge Immoral?' in which, stating his case one Adrian Ross writes: *'A guileless girl, staying at a country house of intimate friends, it appears, was asked to play bridge; she declined, not knowing the game, but was promised advice and yielded. After sundry rubbers, she went to bed; but was informed next morning that she had lost an amount variously stated as from sixty to a hundred pounds.'* The outcome was that her father was called for, the debt paid, and the girl *'removed from the haunt of vice'.*

In the same decade, baccarat, a French gambling game played with cards on a specially designed table was almost obligatory for the fashionable country house party hostess. The Prince of Wales (the future Edward VII) was a particular fan of this illegal game, and until the scandal at Tranby Croft where Sir William Gordon-Cumming, a fellow guest, was accused of cheating and subsequently prosecuted, the Prince always carried his own set of counters ready for an impromptu hand.

A MUSICAL EVENING WILL ADD GREATLY TO ANY HOUSE PARTY

THE FULL-BLOWN MUSICAL EVENING
WAS A FORMAL AFFAIR, INCLUDING
SUPPER, AS FOR A BALL, BUT MUSIC
MIGHT ALSO BE PLAYED MORE
CASUALLY FOLLOWING DINNER.

In a large house, a musical evening
might involve performance in one
room, whilst noisy partying carried on
elsewhere. For a smaller, less formal
affair, guests would simply find places
for themselves near the piano or other
instrument. Conversation was permitted,
but good taste dictated that loud remarks
and laughter were to be avoided. In
houses with galleries above the dining

IN OTHER ROOMS
**Instructing hostesses on dealing with large numbers
of guests dispersed in adjacent rooms,** *Cassell's
Household Guide* **said:** *'... all conversation is not
restrained when music commences; only those within
earshot of the performers are compelled by courtesy
to keep silence. In the adjoining rooms conversation
has full sway, and although a distant murmur may
penetrate to the music-room, listeners are not supposed
to be disturbed by it.'*

- Guests are greeted by the hostess, remaining in position until all have arrived.
- The rustling of programmes and tapping of fans are the only forms of applause permitted to ladies. On no account should they say 'bravo'.
- Sacred music is not appropriate at evening parties. If any is included it should be during the first part of the evening. Chamber music is best suited to a drawing room.
- The question of whether guests will perform at a musical evening should be settled by the hostess before the event.
- It is a compliment to professional performers to ask them to remain for any amusements that may follow.

In the 18th century the Duke of Chandos, friend of the composer Handel, was so enthusiastic about music that he lodged an entire 27-piece orchestra at his house at Canons Park north west of London.

room, music might be played whilst guests were dining.

Advice for performers

Well-educated girls of the family invariably learned the piano and were expected to play – and sing too. Should any lady guest sing or play, and be asked to do so by her hostess, the gentleman nearest to her was expected to escort her to the piano, help her to arrange her music and make sure that her gloves, fan and handkerchief were taken care of. For the hesitant *Enquire Within* advised: 'If you sing well, make no previous excuses: if indifferently, do not hesitate when you are asked, for few people are judges of singing, but everyone is sensible of the desire to please.'

EMBROIDERY IS A SKILL AND TASTE MUCH TO BE DESIRED

A LEISURE ACTIVITY FOR COUNTRY HOUSE LADIES –
AND A PRACTICAL NECESSITY FOR THEIR STAFF.

As well as being decorative, embroidery had practical purposes for mistresses and their daughters, such as decorating personal items of clothing. Below stairs, needlework was a duty of the upper housemaid, carried out under the housekeeper's direction, for the lady's maid and the housekeeper herself.

'Light or fancy needlework', said Mrs Beeton, often formed 'a portion of evening recreation for the ladies of the household'. They might trim and decorate garments, adding their personal monograms, make useful items such as mats, antimacassars and table runners, or create decorative samplers to be hung in bedrooms. To make it easier to see her work by candle or lamplight an embroiderer often had a large mirror on a stand placed strategically behind her to reflect light on to her work.

STAYING IN FASHION

Ladies' maids invariably spent much time altering and embellishing garments to keep up with changing styles and fashions, and even trimming hats. In large households, sewing of all kinds might be put out to women in a nearby village, or taken on by a maid hired – often from France or Switzerland – specifically for the role.

HELP FOR THE NEEDLE

By Victorian times, ready-printed designs for embroideries were available, a trend denigrated by *Cassell's Household Guide* which insisted that *'this absence of invention and good taste'* was *'neither necessary nor desirable'*. Advocating a return to *'the beautiful occupation of their female ancestors'* the manual expressed the view that *'there is at the present time much desire for this shown among the upper classes, and legitimate embroidery is again rapidly becoming a fashionable employment.'*

A COUNTRY HOUSE BALL IS A WELCOME DIVERSION

ONCE NOBILITY AND GENTRY WERE ABLE TO TRAVEL WITH REASONABLE EASE AND BEGAN TO SOCIALIZE, PRIVATE COUNTRY HOUSE BALLS BECAME REGULAR ENTERTAINMENTS.

A GRACEFUL DANCE

Edward Austen-Leigh, nephew of Jane Austen brought the minuet to life: *'The stately minuet reigned supreme; and every regular ball commenced with it. It was a slow and solemn movement, expressive of grace and dignity, rather than of merriment. It abounded in formal bows and curtsies, with measured paces, forwards, backwards and sideways, and many complicated gyrations.'*

From the 16th century, guests at country house balls ranged from local friends to royalty. The earliest balls took on a distinct pattern, beginning with dinner, which might be accompanied by music. Guests then retired to the drawing room for dessert, to drink tea and possibly play cards before returning to the dining room for dancing. To ensure that guests did not return home hungry, yet more food was proffered at the end of the evening. And to assist coachmen bringing guests to and from balls, dates were deliberately arranged to coincide with the full moon to help them find their way more easily along country lanes.

Popular dances

By the 18th century, the most popular dances included the hornpipe, various reels and the minuet, a formal and difficult dance. As the century progressed, balls became ever more elaborate with masquerades, to which guests wore masks, and *ridottos* which were combinations of dances and concerts.

At ball-assemblies dancing was combined with activities such as card playing which carried on, with an all-evening supper, in different rooms of the house. By the Victorian era the grand supper ball was the height of fashion, with dancing in the ballroom, if there was one, and with dances including the quadrille, which according to etiquette was danced by the lady of the house to open proceedings.

ENSURING SUCCESS

Good music was indispensable to the success of a ball. *'The pianoforte'*, said *Cassell's Household Guide*, *'is not sufficient…'* It also commented on the serving of food, advising that *'It is imperative that any viands that have been cut should be replaced by fresh ones for succeeding visitors'*; and that to leave some of the company *'to fare as best as they can from remnants would be the height of ill manners.'*

A SERVANT'S BALL OR DINNER SHOULD BE HELD AT LEAST ONCE A YEAR

IN LARGE HOUSEHOLDS, A BALL OR GRAND DINNER FOR SERVANTS AND TENANTS ON THE ESTATE, WOULD BE HELD AT LEAST ONCE A YEAR, USUALLY ON TWELFTH NIGHT.

To display their generosity, good masters and mistresses – and members of the family – even turned the tables and waited on their servants, as well as providing bountiful fare. At Tredegar House near Newport the annual servants' balls, held on Twelfth Night, were famous in the area and attended by estate workers and local suppliers as well as household staff. If he was in residence Lord Tredegar would have the first dance with the housekeeper before leaving to allow everyone to enjoy the evening.

Even after his Lordship had retired to bed, a band played on into the early hours, the party finishing at about 5.30 in the morning, although some staff were due to begin work only half an hour later. A huge buffet was laid out in the great kitchen and wine and beer freely supplied. Not surprisingly many servants met their future spouses at the balls, when they had the opportunity to relax and dance resplendent in their best clothes.

In some houses less formal monthly dances were organized, with staff playing musical instruments. Popular Edwardian dances ranged from quadrilles, waltzes and polkas to country dances.

A great feast

At Hatfield House in the 1890s the Cecil family provided each New Year, a 'tenantry dinner' consisting, so the records note of 'two hundred and seventy-six meat dishes, forty-eight pie dishes and salts.' Three dozen butter boats and 500 plates were needed for the occasion, which was marked with a speech by the landlord.

AT A WEDDING BREAKFAST FLOWERS MAY ABOUND EVERYWHERE

FLOWERS WERE CERTAINLY ESSENTIAL, BUT IT WAS
IMPORTANT THAT THEY DID NOT MAR THE COMFORT OR
CONVERSATION OF GUESTS SEATED AT THE TABLE.

A country house wedding ceremony took place in the chapel of the house or in a nearby church, usually in the morning, and was followed by a wedding breakfast in the middle of the day. As today, the wedding cake was displayed with a decorative floral surround. Wedding gifts would be received at the house several days before the event and, as was deemed polite, displayed in the drawing room on the day for all to see.

The order of going to church was as today, with the bridegroom – in morning dress – waiting at the church for the bride who, accompanied by her father, was the last to leave the house. Modesty demanded that her dress was simple, with long sleeves and a high neck.

The wedding breakfast

On return from the ceremony, all participants sat down to a wedding breakfast, which was very similar to a ball supper. Delights included stewed oysters, galantines, mayonnaise of fowl, lobster patties, cold game, jellies, creams and all the grand designs of confectionery. Iced desserts were handed round at the end of the meal.

A DAY OFF IS AN OPPORTUNITY FOR A FAMILY REUNION

FOR SERVANTS FORTUNATE ENOUGH TO BE ALLOWED SUFFICIENT TIME OFF, ESPECIALLY IF THEY WERE YOUNG, REUNITING WITH THE FAMILY, WAS VITAL.

As a rule, younger and more junior country house servants were hired from nearby farms, villages and towns. This made family visits possible although these might entail walking considerable distances. In benign households the cook ensured that a maid was given a basket of food such as preserves, cold meat and cakes to take with her. Hours off were also the chance for couples to walk and talk together, and to progress through the rituals of courtship away from the prying eyes of the 'big house'.

Pastimes and games

When leisure time was spent in the house many staff enjoyed playing musical instruments such as fiddles. In some establishments a piano was provided in the servants'

An annual 'must'
Even if days off during the year were sparse, Mothering Sunday, the fourth Sunday in Lent, was the one day of the year on which girls in service were always allowed home to visit their families.

Writing in 1759 the owner of an estate remarked that: *'In the village where I live we have five public-houses, two of which have Nine-pin grounds and shuffleboards... our livery servants neglect their household and other services, to spend their time at those houses.'* **Cards and dancing were other attractions of the public house.**

hall. Spare time might also be spent sewing and knitting, reading the penny novelettes of the day, and similar domestic pursuits. The local pub was also a place of entertainment.

Outdoors, male staff might take part in cricket matches organized by the master of the house or in a village. The Duchess of Portland, knowledgeable regarding the value of fresh air and exercise, presented each of her footmen with a bicycle and a set of golf clubs. Indoors, staff were often encouraged to join in family theatricals and concerts.

IT IS POSSIBLE FOR FRIENDS TO BE ENTERTAINED BELOW STAIRS

DEPENDING ON THE STRICTNESS OF THE REGIME, STAFF COULD RECEIVE CALLS FROM FRIENDS AND RELATIVES ON DAYS OFF AND AT LESS BUSY TIMES DURING THE DAY.

During such visits, staff would talk, drink tea – or ale if available – and play cards. Meals might also be taken. In country houses with large staffs, firm friendships were formed, especially between those of similar ages such as maids, who often shared the same bedroom. Social life was more difficult for 'upper' servants who were discouraged from fraternizing with the lower orders and, where houses were remotely situated, grooms and under-gardeners habitually helped out in the pantry in the evenings purely for the company.

GARDEN AND GROUNDS

Defining the 'English Gentleman' in 1890 Daniel Defoe said that he should have 'venison perhaps in his park, sufficient for his own table at least ... pigeons from a dove-house in the yard, fish in his own ponds or in some small river adjoining, and within his own royalty' plus 'all the needful addenda to his kitchen, which a small dairy of four or five cows yields to him.' This made him, at the very least, a most important local employer, if not a smallholder or even a farmer.

The evolving garden

The way in which the country house garden and grounds were arranged changed and developed with the centuries. So while the Tudor garden was embellished with formal knot gardens and the like, and the 17th-century house and park separated from each other by a terrace, the designers of the 19th century removed the barriers between the two, opening up the landscape, making the whole look much more natural, and adding eye-catching features such as follies and temples.

A diversity of activities

While the flower garden provided a supply of blooms for decorating the house, in the kitchen garden the head gardener needed to cultivate fruit and vegetables for year-round use and, with the help of glasshouses and heating, grow the exotic items so prized by country house owners. The grounds also needed facilities for brewing and an ice house, as well as space for stabling horses, the safe keeping of carriages and, in later eras, the garaging for motor cars. Important staff members such as gamekeepers had their own residences on the estate, while grooms lived over the stables.

THE HEAD GARDENER MUST UNDERSTAND THE ELEMENTS OF LANDSCAPING

A VITAL ASPECT OF THE COUNTRY HOUSE GARDEN, BUT PARTICULARLY IN THE AGE OF THE GREAT DESIGNERS LANCELOT 'CAPABILITY' BROWN AND HIS SUCCESSOR HUMPHREY REPTON.

The country house owner, keen to improve the look of his land would, if he did not employ a specialist such as Brown, rely on his head gardener to come up with suggestions for laying out walks, devising views (known as 'prospects') arranging features such as urns, obelisks and benches, and rigging up fountains and other waterworks. It is no coincidence that the landscape movement coincided with the Acts of Enclosure, passed between 1730 and 1820, which allowed landowners to formalize the separation of agricultural and park land.

'Capability' Brown earned his nickname from his skill of exploring an estate to assess its 'capabilities' or potential. His aim was for a beauty that blotted out nature's imperfections to create an air of serenity. Under his supervision, as at locations such as Croome Court in Worcestershire, where he also advised on the creation of the house itself, hills were levelled, lakes dug and grottoes created. To shape garden contours, Brown planted huge numbers of trees.

WELL QUALIFIED

A gardener advertising for a position in the *Bristol Gazette* in 1773 was careful to state that he understood *'laying out Ground Work, in the modern Taste, perfectly well....'*

Repton's Red Book

Many of the great British landowners of the early 19th century employed the skills of Humphrey Repton who prepared for each client a Red Book, illustrating in beautiful watercolour the effect he intended to produce. He cleverly adapted many of Capability Brown's creations, adding sinuous drives that provided intermittent glimpses of the house on approach, and linking house and grounds with terraces and beds of ornamental flowers chosen to bloom in different seasons.

THE WATER PAVILION: WREST: BEDFORDSHIRE

Repton's Gardens

The many country house gardens designed to great effect by Humphrey Repton included:

• Woburn Abbey, Bedforshire: Notable for its flower corridor, a rosary, an American garden (to display new introductions) and a Chinese garden – and its menagerie.

• Endsleigh, near Tavistock, Devon: The land around the Tamar Valley landscaped around a *cottage orné*, a sporting lodge built by Jeffry Wyatville.

• Plas Newydd, North Wales: Repton re-designed the drive and planted more trees between the house and the stables, so that on approaching the house it was impossible to see both buildings at once. The home farm was moved farther from the house to the south-west, next to the orchard.

• Ashridge, Surrey: The garden for which the 'mixed style' was first advocated, by Repton in his 1813 *Red Book*. After Repton's death, his proposals for 15 different types of garden were adapted and implemented by Sir Jeffry Wyatville. Features include an Italian garden, a circular rose garden, a monk's garden and Holy Well, an Armorial Garden, a conservatory, a grotto and an avenue of Wellingtonias leading to an arboretum.

THE IMPRESSION OF ANY HOUSE, WHEN SEEN FROM A DISTANCE, IS ENHANCED BY A HA-HA

THE HA-HA, A SUNKEN WALL AND DITCH, WAS A KEY ELEMENT OF THE NATURALISTIC MOVEMENT OF THE 18TH CENTURY AND BECAME A STANDARD FEATURE OF THE ENGLISH COUNTRY HOUSE GARDEN.

As well as being an invisible barrier keeping animals such as sheep and cows confined to their pastures, the ha-ha allowed uninterrupted views from the house to the park or from the park to the surrounding countryside. The ha-ha was the inspiration of the garden designer Charles Bridgeman (1690–1738), who brought it from France. Bridgeman was instrumental in the move away from geometric Tudor layouts and working on Lord Cobham's estate he installed a ha-ha at Stowe in around 1714. Bridgeman's contribution was, however, overshadowed by that of his contemporary William Kent (1685–1748), the painter, architect and founder of the English landscape tradition.

About the name

Ha-has are believed to be named from the exclamations of surprise uttered by anyone encountering one. They vary in depth from about 60 cm (2 ft) at Horton House in Northants to 2.7 m (9 ft) at Petworth House in West Sussex.

William Kent's masterpiece was Rousham in Oxfordshire where he created vistas out towards the river Cherwell as well as woodland walks and open glades, each ending in a 'surprise' architectural feature.

At houses such as Charlecote in Warwickshire the ha-ha was also installed to create the illusion that deer could wander right up to the house.

The Victorian view

By the Victorian era, reaction had set in against the landscape movement. The designers Humphrey Repton and William Gilpin argued that: 'If it be contrary to good sense to admit the cattle on the dressed lawn, it is, I conceive, equally contrary to let it appear they are

admitted.' As a result, garden walls, fences and 'see-through' iron railings were erected and the flower garden returned to the immediate environs of the house. Terraces, which had been removed a century earlier were reinstated, marking the separation between house and park.

EVERY SIZEABLE GARDEN IS IN NEED OF HERBACEOUS BORDERS

THE HERBACEOUS BORDER CAME INTO ITS OWN IN THE VICTORIAN ERA, AND THE LARGE COUNTRY HOUSE GARDEN WAS A PERFECT SETTING FOR MAGNIFICENT DISPLAYS.

Wherever borders were placed in the garden – particularly when surrounding shrubberies or creating borders beside grassy walks – mixing colours was all important. The amateur gardener Shirley Hibberd (1825 – 90) recommended a repetition of plant or colour groups placed at intervals along a mixed border. 'The hardy herbaceous

BEAUTIFUL BORDERS

'In many situations near houses, and especially old houses' says William Robinson in *The English Flower Garden* of 1883 *'there are delightful opportunities for a very beautiful kind of flower border…. Here we can have the best soil and keep it for our favourites.'* Among the many specimens he recommended for the mixed border were delphiniums, lilies, peonies and irises.

border' he said in antithesis to single-species plantings, 'is the best feature of the flower garden... When well made, well stocked and well managed, it presents us with flowers in abundance during ten months of twelve... while the bedding system is an embellishment, the herbaceous border is a fundamental feature.'

Designer influences

By the early 20th century the herbaceous border had not only been accepted but developed, particularly as a result of the influence of Gertrude Jekyll (1843–1932), who also incorporated shrubby plants such as sage into the herbaceous border to provide 'filler' foliage. Her many designs, which always paid great attention to colour, included seasonal borders placed in different locations in the garden.

A HEAD GARDENER IS AN INDIVIDUAL OF NO LITTLE IMPORTANCE

FOR THIS POSITION HE ALSO NEEDED TO BE EDUCATED AND POSSESS CONSIDERABLE PRACTICAL KNOWLEDGE.

The head gardener of a country house certainly had to be versatile. For as well as attending to beds and borders he had to manage greenhouses, hot houses and conservatories, and grow fruit and vegetables. He needed to know about landscaping and design, soils and composts and be an expert in propagating all kinds of plants, including shrubs and trees. There were also ponds, lakes and water gardens to maintain year round, plus lawns, which required constant attention, especially if used for tennis and croquet.

GARDEN PLEASANTRIES

The head gardener needed to be pleasant and courteous, since he regularly showed visitors around the garden. *'Take every opportunity'*, **said Anthony Heasel in his 18th-century guide,** *'of entertaining those who come to visit your master, with a particular description of every thing in the garden, and have always some places ready for them to rest themselves on, while passing from one part to another.'*

THE GARDEN TEAM
The intensive labour of the garden – digging, trenching, mowing, gravelling, hoeing and the like – was performed by a team of under gardeners. In a large estate they might number as many as 25. In common with head gardeners the most senior of these would live in cottages on the grounds. As a perk many were given free wood for fires to heat their homes.

With the seasons

With training as an under gardener, and with experience, the head gardener could learn how to perform each garden operation in the right season, and with an eye to the weather. In spring and autumn, walls and buildings in the garden needed to be repaired and painted, if necessary, and tools properly cleaned and sharpened. The 'basic' set of tools in the mid 19th century included: spade, shovel, rake, hoe, fork (three pronged), trowel, shears, scythe, pruning knife, hay rake, dibber, line and reel, besom and garden roller.

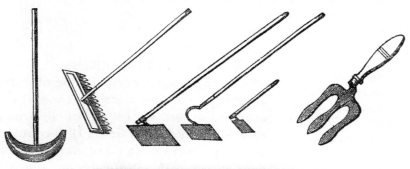

TIPS FOR THE HEAD GARDENER

Some 19th-century advice for head gardeners that still holds good.
• Complete every part of an operation as you proceed.
• Finish one job before beginning another.
• In passing to and from the work, or on any occasion … keep a vigilant look out for weeds, decayed leaves, or any other deformity and remove them.
• Let no crop of fruit, or herbaceous vegetables, go to waste on the spot.
• Cut down the flower stalks of all plants.
• Keep every part of what is under your care, perfect in its kind.

DECORATIVE FEATURES DESERVE A PROMINENT PLACE IN THE COUNTRY HOUSE GARDEN

THE COUNTRY HOUSE GARDEN COULD CONTAIN ANY MANNER OF DECORATIVE FEATURES FROM STATUES AND OBELISKS TO GARDEN FOLLIES AND TEMPLES.

Statues found their place in the English garden in the late 16th century and in country house gardens they were particularly enjoyed as, said John Woolridge in 1677, a 'Winter diversion ... to recompense the loss of past pleasures, and to buoy up hope of another Spring'. Since stone and marble quickly became prey to the weather, sculptures began to be made in lead, often painted to resemble marble or bronze.

A building craze

The craze for follies really took off in the 1690s, with such eccentric constructions as the gigantic 'pineapple' built at Dunmore Park near Falkirk in Scotland. Towers were also popular, and could be climbed to admire the view. At Dallington in Sussex the local squire swore to his dinner guests that he could see the tower of the village church from his window. When this proved impossible, he promptly built a pyramid dubbed the Sugar Loaf on his own land, with its pointed peak as high as the church spire.

A POET'S INSCRIPTION

At Stourhead a marble slab in the Grotto bears an inscription translated from the Latin of Cardinal Bembo (1470–1547) by the poet Alexander Pope (1688–1744) that reads: '*Nymph of the Grot these sacred springs I keep; and to the murmur of these waters sleep; Ah! Spare my slumbers, gently tread the cave; And drink in silence or in silence lave.*' Much dulled over the centuries, the inscription is currently being restored.

With a purpose

A garden feature sometimes had a purpose beyond pure ornament. The gardens of Elizabethan and Jacobean times often sported banqueting houses built, as at Hardwick Hall in Derbyshire, in the style of roof turrets. At Blickling in Norfolk, however, the banqueting house was a mock Medieval design.

LEAD VASE AT HAMPTON COURT.

Adding atmosphere

As the English landscape garden evolved, so eye-catching features were introduced to add atmosphere and interest to the 'living picture' that was the garden. In some gardens, as at Stowe in Buckinghamshire, the features were specifically placed to mark stages in a garden perambulation. Its massive Doric arch, for instance, framed a view of the garden's Palladian bridge. And at Stourhead in Wiltshire, the garden Pantheon is sited at the focal point of the view from the hillside near the house.

BOX AND YEW ARE THE MOST USEFUL PLANTS FOR HEDGING AND TOPIARY

LONG USED IN KNOT GARDENS, FRAGRANT BOX WAS AN IDEAL PLANT FOR CLIPPING INTO SMALL SHAPES; YEW WAS PREFERRED FOR TALLER EFFECTS.

In Tudor times, almost every country house garden included a knot garden created by interweaving box with herbs into a beautiful pattern. Low box hedges were also used to edge beds and borders, including rose beds. To keep it looking good, box needed an annual clipping in late May or early June, once it had started into growth, which is when topiary shapes could best be created. Care was also needed to keep the foliage of other plants well clear, for aesthetic reasons and to prevent disease. Box 'balls' for formal garden designs were made by training plants or by grafting between species.

TOPIARY WORK AT LEVENS HALL : WESTMORELAND

THE ART OF TOPIARY

Yews were used for hedging and as specimen trees planted, for instance, in pairs at the top of garden steps. Clipping yew into shapes became the rage in the 19th century when bird forms were especially favoured, echoing the live creatures of the dovecote.

While yew topiary was the passion of many Victorian gardeners, William Robinson thought it an abomination, declaring even unfussy clipping as a 'misuse' not only in British gardens but even at Versailles.

WATER FEATURES PROVIDE ENDLESS OPPORTUNITIES FOR HORTICULTURAL EMBELLISHMENT

AS LONG AS THEY WERE WELL MAINTAINED, AND PREVENTED FROM BECOMING STAGNANT AND SMELLY, WATER FEATURES MADE A DELIGHTFUL ADDITION TO THE COUNTRY HOUSE GARDEN.

Water gardens could be anything from informal streams, bordered with flowers and trailing shrubs, to large lakes. Among the most beautiful was the canal garden at Bridge House in Surrey, designed by the landscape architect Harold Peto. Here a lily pond ornamented with hydrangeas sits alongside a pillared pergola festooned with climbers.

Spectacular design

Where there was water there were also spouts, cascades and fountains. In hilly

Garden amusement

There was fun to be had with water features, as at Enstone in Oxfordshire where, with the help of mechanical devices, water flowed to sounds such as the song of a nightingale or the beating of a drum and a 'canopy of rain' formed creating a rainbow.

THE FISHPOND : WREST : BEDFORDSHIRE

locations such as Chatsworth in Derbyshire, water 'staircases' were created in the early 18th century. Here, water gushed from a cascade house out of the mouths of beasts, pipes and urns, and, said Daniel Defoe, 'a whole river descends the slope of a hill a quarter of a mile in length, over steps, with a terrible noise, and broken appearance.' The design most favoured for fountains was the three-tiered *compotière* whose shape was mirrored indoors in everything from candelabra to flower arrangements.

GARDEN FLOWERS ARE REQUIRED FOR INDOOR ARRANGEMENTS

FLORAL DECORATIONS WERE ALWAYS ESSENTIAL FOR THE DINING TABLE, FOR THE HALL AND OTHER ROOMS IN THE HOUSE.

Supplying flowers year round was the responsibility of the head gardener and his assistants. Roses were essential for indoor arrangements and, given good selection of outdoor varieties, could be in bloom from late spring right through until autumn. Some were even forced for February blooming. In spring, tulips and other bulbs such as hyacinths were used indoors, but even more important were lilies which, grown under glass or in a 'reserve garden' would ideally have been available all year.

For perfect blooms

Among the other 'florist's flowers' recommended by Robert Thompson were chrysanthemums, raised both outdoors and in, and propagated by cuttings, and carnations which needed to be increased by a technique known as layering. To create large, perfect carnation blooms, circular pieces of card, each with a hole in the centre, were placed over individual buds before they opened. Hollyhocks were also grown for indoor decoration. These were raised in pots before being planted out.

THE SUNDIAL IS AN APPROPRIATE ORNAMENT FOR THE GARDEN

AS WELL AS HAVING A PRACTICAL USE, SUNDIALS BECAME POPULAR GARDEN ORNAMENTS IN COUNTRY HOUSE GARDENS FROM THE LATE 15TH CENTURY ONWARDS.

The move of sundials from church walls into large gardens, where they became constant reminders of the cycle of days, months and seasons, came about as a result of Renaissance advances in accuracy and design. Henry VIII set the trend with more than 20 horizontal and beautifully ornamented sundials ordered by his King's Horologer the Bavarian astronomer and diallist Nicholas Kratzer (c.1487–1550).

The typical sundial of the period consisted of a metal plate on which was mounted the gnomon – also in metal – the arm which cast the shadow to mark the hour. The whole was then mounted on a stone pedestal. Even in the Victorian age, when every country house contained many accurate clocks, garden sundials continued in popularity. In an era that combined practicality with religious fervour and sentimentality, the use of traditional sundial inscriptions remained vital.

SUNDIAL: WREST: BEDFORDSHIRE

SUNDIAL SAYINGS

Many sundials were furnished with family crests and other ornaments and with mottoes, usually in Latin and often religious, reflecting on the passing of time.

Lex Dei lux dei
The law of God is the light of day

Fugit irreparable tempus
Irredeemable time flies away

Umbra sumus
We are a shadow

Noli confidere nocti
Trust not the night

Vulnerant omnes, ultima necat
Every (hour) wounds, the last kills

A huge structure
At Wollaton Hall in Nottinghamshire Robert Smythson installed a massive sundial 3.5 ft (just over a metre) in diameter as the central feature in a parterre. Although the original garden no longer exists there is evidence that it had a separate area devoted entirely to a large sundial collection.

A PERGOLA WALK SHOULD BE IN KEEPING WITH THE MATERIAL OF THE HOUSE

A KEY CONCEPT OF 19TH-CENTURY DESIGN FOR THE COUNTRY HOUSE GARDEN AND ONE ESPOUSED BY SUCH LUMINARIES AS GERTRUDE JEKYLL AND EDWIN LUTYENS.

Tunnel-arbours had been popular features of country house gardens in the 16th century but were revived with enthusiasm towards the end of the 19th using for supports everything from sculptured Doric and Ionic columns reminiscent of Italian gardens to timber (especially oak) and pillars of stone, brick or chalk. For more delicate effects metal frames, originally imported from Germany, were also employed. A scented pergola was a place for home owners and their visitors to stroll at leisure. Simplicity was key to perfection.

Roses, as today, were favourites for clothing the pergola, with 'Gloire de Dijon', bred in France and described in *The English Flower Garden* as 'the most precious flowers that ever adorned the garden', being highly favoured. Vines were also recommended by Robinson, as 'living drapery' as were wisteria, Virginia creeper, honeysuckle, jasmine and clematis.

A pergola to visit

At Aberglasney in Wales it is still possible to walk through the massive, darkly romantic yew tunnel, believed to have been planted in the 18th century, while at Moseley Old Hall in Staffordshire an arbour of hornbeam leads to a tunnel of oak covered with *Clematis viticella* and *C. flammula* and with the claret vine *Vitis vinifera*. The design is based on one illustrated in 1577 in Thomas Hill's *The Gardener's Labyrinth*.

THE CONTINUOUS SUPPLY OF FRESH VEGETABLES IS A VITAL PART OF THE GARDENER'S DUTIES

BEHIND THE HIGH WALLS OF THE KITCHEN GARDEN, ALL MANNER OF VEGETABLES WERE GROWN IN SUCCESSION TO KEEP THE HOUSE WELL FED THROUGHOUT THE YEAR.

Until the early 18th century, flowers and vegetables were often decoratively planted together in parterres and 'pleasure gardens', but then became separated, often on a large scale. The planting plan was devised to allow for crop rotation and to ensure that crops needing the most warmth, such as winter lettuces and early carrots, occupied the sunniest, most sheltered positions. For forcing outside the greenhouse, glass cloches were placed over vegetables such as salads.

Members of the cabbage family were given particular attention in the kitchen garden, as were peas, beans and spinach. While the head gardener welcomed the mistress of the house or her daughters to choose fruit such as grapes for an embellishment, he would always prefer to pick produce himself. Ladies who valued their gardeners were advised to 'humour this weakness'.

VERSATILE BEANS

Remarking on the culinary value of beans Robert Thompson says that: *'If the green pods are superabundant in summer, they may be preserved in salt, for use in winter; they may be made into a pickle alone, or together with other vegetables; and, finally, the ripe seed can be used in a variety of ways, in haricots, soups, and stews.'*

Peas and beans

Country house gardeners across England strove to have peas ready for the table by June 4th, the birthday of King George III, and a crop was even grown for the Christmas table by planting them in pots in the autumn then raising them in a heated greenhouse for the next couple of months.

The beans most commonly grown in country house gardens were varieties of broad beans, which were podded and eaten as a valuable source of protein, although for fine dining very small beans were required. As with peas, successional sowing was necessary to extend the season as much as possible. Brown, red and green Windsor were among the most favoured varieties, Windsor being particularly well suited to soup making. Also popular – and versatile – were kidney beans, which could also be eaten young, and green French beans.

WALLS PROVIDE A PERFECT PROTECTION FOR FRUIT TREES

THE WALLED KITCHEN GARDEN WAS PARTICULARLY SUITED TO THE GROWING OF ESPALIERED OR CORDONED FRUIT TREES.

PROTECTION FROM WIND

As Sir Robert Stapleton, a 16th-century Yorkshire landowner recorded: *'... if you defend not your orchard from the northerly and easterly wind you can never have dainty fruit... It is convenient to defend your orchard from the wind on all sides, otherwise your apples & other fruits will be cast down often times ere they be ripe.'*

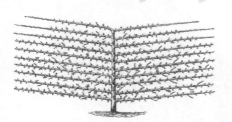

Walls, which gained great popularity in 18th and 19th centuries, provided the perfect way to protect outdoor crops. The traditional arrangement of the large walled country house garden was to divide it into four, with each quarter again divided into four, and with a fruit tree in the centre. Apples and gooseberries might be planted around the borders of each quarter with espaliered or cordoned fruit against the high walls, including apples, pears, plums, quinces, nectarines and cherries.

The walls not only served to keep out rabbits, deer and other 'pests' but, because they warmed up during the day and released their heat gradually during the night, they kept fruit at an even temperature.

ADDING HEAT

For growing tender Mediterranean fruit such as peaches and the apricot 'Moorpark', a highly fragrant variety, and for cultivating outdoor vines, south facing walls were not only made extra thick but were heated by fireplaces built into their backs. Heat was conducted through flues set into the brickwork.

RARE AND UNUSUAL PLANTS MAY BE KEPT IN A CONSERVATORY

EXOTIC SPECIMENS OF ALL KINDS THRIVED IN THE COUNTRY HOUSE CONSERVATORY, WHICH COULD EITHER BE FREESTANDING OR ATTACHED TO THE HOUSE.

From the early 18th century, when conservatories were first built for the wealthiest country houses, construction was from brick or stone and designs rectangular. Glass panes – at that time extremely costly – were small and numerous.

Conservatories became hugely popular following the completion of Joseph Paxton's Great Conservatory at Chatsworth in 1841, built specifically to house the giant Amazonian water lily, and his Crystal Palace, constructed for the Great Exhibition in 1851. The Victorians favoured

ESSENTIAL WARMTH

Additional heat for the conservatory was provided by a stove. However the gardener needed to know whether the plants in his care demanded dry or moist heat, and adjust the system accordingly.

Advising in *The Gardener's Assistant* Robert Thompson says: *'Bottom heat for stoves is sometimes supplied by means of tanners' bark placed in a pit in the body of the house, and on this the pots containing plants are set, or occasionally plunged in it, to a greater or lesser depth, as when it is necessary to excite their roots more than their tops. But generally a fair share of bottom heat is maintained by placing the pots on slate or stone, under which there is a heated chamber, whether by flues, hot-water pipes, tanks, or heated air; but hot-water pipes are the most eligible.'*

hexagonal or round shapes with steep roofs; panes were large and design details included glass fanlights, bay windows, arched doorways, and elegant cast iron eave brackets.

A veritable 'jungle'

Inside the conservatory, favourite plants massed together included abutilons; jasmines; fuchsias; heliotropes; palms; aspidistras; and ferns of all kinds including maidenhair, holly and Boston ferns. Within this 'jungle', which became ever more exotic as plant hunters brought new species from distant lands, might be a pool with water ferns, water lilies and fish, and even a fountain. Chairs, tables and bench designs favoured by the Victorians were of cast iron, mimicking the shapes of tree trunks and roots with 'foliage' embellishments.

ACCESS TO THE HOUSE

The conservatory often opened direct into the drawing room or might serve as a means of disguising the servants' wing of the house, with an opening into the hall. Alternatively, as at Mentmore in Buckinghamshire, it might link the morning and smoking rooms.

HEAT IS ALWAYS REQUIRED FOR GROWING EXOTIC FRUIT

A SAYING PARTICULARLY TRUE FOR ORANGES BUT ALSO
FOR PRIZED EXOTIC FRUITS SUCH AS PINEAPPLES, WHICH
WERE FREQUENTLY CULTIVATED AT COUNTRY HOUSES.

In northern Europe, the first orangeries such as the one at Dyrham Park in Gloucestershire built in 1702, had solid roofs but these were replaced by glass a century later. Couples who wanted to be together but out of sight, relished the confines of the orangery for clandestine meetings.

As well as oranges, lemons and limes were grown in the orangery while vines, peaches, apricots, plums, figs and cherries were cultivated under glass in large houses with sloping glass roofs reaching down to ground level. Peach trees might be mixed with vines. Both figs and cherries were planted in pots, although figs also thrived if set direct into a border.

Ingenious structures

For protecting pineapples and melons – and out of season vegetable fruits such as cucumbers – elaborate pits were constructed, heated by hot water pipes from below and by the sun from above, entering through a sloping glass

COAXING EARLY FRUIT

To ensure a supply of fruit early in the season, trees needed heat to coax them into life in mid winter. Once the buds broke, constant attention was necessary for, as the 1862 *Book of Garden Management* **said:** *'From the time the bud bursts its horny sheath until the luscious fruit melts in your mouth, all work and no play – all growth and no check, must be the stern regimen of the successful cultivator.'*

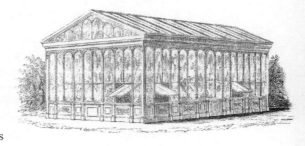

roof. Beneath the plants was a chamber into which rotting manure from the stables was inserted to 'supply moisture and ammonia', which also helped to deter insect pests. Plant roots might also be allowed to penetrate – and benefit from – this rich compost. Good ventilation was essential, particularly for fruits such as plums and cherries needing insect pollination.

SUCCESSFUL PROPAGATION

For early pickings of redcurrants, gooseberries and raspberries, plants were potted up in late winter and brought on with even warmth in heated glasshouses. For strawberries at Christmas, plants were propagated then raised in pits in the same way as pineapples.

AN ICE HOUSE MUST BE SITUATED IN A SPOT SUFFICIENTLY ELEVATED TO ALLOW COMPLETE DRAINAGE

A FEATURE OF COUNTRY HOUSE ESTATES FROM THE 17TH CENTURY, ICE HOUSES NEEDED TO BE CONSTRUCTED SO AS TO KEEP THE CONTENTS USEABLE FOR MANY MONTHS ON END.

The side of a north-facing slope was the ideal position for an ice house, with a door facing south east. The alternative – as in the earliest examples – was to dig a pit and line it with bricks. In either case, drainage was essential so that water could run away through a grating, plus an air trap, to prevent warm air getting in and melting the ice. Damp was even more of a problem, especially in ice houses constructed on water-retaining clay and loam. Those built on free-draining chalk and gravel were undoubtedly the most effective. Keeping the ice house away from trees was also important because, although shade providers, their roots were a source of damp.

Essential insulation

Good insulation was vital. This was provided by constructing double walls, with insulation such as sawdust between them, and by covering the roof with straw thatch. On top of this might be placed earth planted over with ivy. Barley straw was also used in layers between two or three doors, put into canvas bags to make it easier to manage.

Filling the ice house was an annual task, but it was topped up as the opportunity arose. Until the 1800s, ice was collected from lakes on the estate and from specially constructed shallow 'freezing pools'. In southern counties, compacted snow was commonly used in its place.

Ice from abroad

From 1842, when the first shipment of ice from Fresh Pond, Boston, arrived in Britain on the barque *Shannon* a better, purer form of ice was available. The Wenham Lake Company set up offices in London and organized the distribution of this superior ice to estates around the country. Later, Norwegian ice was also

THE USES OF SNOW
Robert Copeman, the steward of Blickling Hall in Norfolk recorded in April 1790 that: *'There was a great fall of snow this afternoon, as soon as ever it was thick enough I spoke to the Gardeners and had as many Labourers as I could. The ice house is about half full; the men kept at it between 9 & 10 o'clock.'*

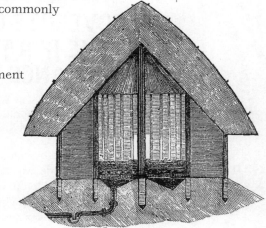

available. Although considered poorer in quality, it was
available through the summer months when most needed.

THE PRICE OF ICE

Quoting prices of ice from the USA, *Cassell's
Household Guide* **says that:** *'American ice is sold by
many ice dealers at about 7s. per 100 lbs.; 3s 6d. per
50 lbs.; 2s per 25 lbs.; and in any smaller quantity at
2d per lb.; and is packed in a mat or blanket, for the
country at a further charge of 2s per 100 lbs; and in
larger quantity at some reduction in this rate.'*

KEEPING FOOD COOL

Food was sometimes stored in the ice house, but more usually ice was removed
as needed and placed in ice boxes and chests in the kitchen where it was used
for refrigeration and for cooling ices and other cold dishes.

NO DOVECOTE CAN POSSIBLY SURVIVE IF RATS HAVE FOUND AN ENTRANCE TO IT

ONE VERY GOOD REASON WHY DOVECOTES HAVE LONG
BEEN PLACED WELL ABOVE GROUND. THE OLDEST
DESIGNS ARE ROUND OR SHAPED LIKE BEEHIVES.

Building a dovecote, which might house hundreds or even
thousands of birds, was originally a privilege of the lord of
the manor and forbidden to his tenants – a practice that led to
many complaints since the birds were free to ravage the crops
of tenant farmers. Doves and pigeons were an important

DOVECOTE HYGIENE

The manure or tillage from the dovecote, prized as a fertilizer, was removed twice a year in November and the end of February. Hygiene was vital since, as *Cassell's Household Guide* **advises:** *'The young of the dove-cote pigeon, like all others of the columbine order are reared in a nest lined by their own dung, which if left in the hole after the birds are gone is apt to harbour vermin... They will destroy every young pigeon within their reach.'*

source of meat and eggs for the country house, particularly in winter when other fresh ingredients were hard to come by; the young birds known as squabs or squeakers were the greatest delicacies.

Designed for access

The distinctive cupola set atop many dovecotes, often equipped with landing ledges and sheltered perches, made it easy for birds to go in and out. Within, internal shutters might be fitted, or even dormer windows. Simpler versions had ledges placed around the exterior in front of the entrance and exit holes. Small compartments within cotes of all sizes ensured ideal nesting conditions. Each pair of birds might, in a lifetime of seven years, produce two or more chicks twice a year.

POSITIONING AND MAINTENANCE
In country house grounds, dovecotes were often placed near poultry and near the bakehouse, brewhouse and stables. Since the birds needed plentiful supplies of water the cotes were also put close to fishponds. To encourage birds to stay in a new dovecote the floor was sprinkled with a strong smelling substance such as asafoetida, a pungent spice related to fennel.

BREWING BEER IS EXCLUSIVELY CONFINED TO HOUSEHOLDS IN THE COUNTRY

MANY COUNTRY ESTABLISHMENTS HAD BREW HOUSES
SPECIFICALLY FOR THIS PURPOSE. IN SMALLER ONES
BEER WAS MADE IN THE SCULLERY WITH LAUNDRY TUBS
DOUBLING AS BREWING TUNS.

The tradition of brewing beer grew up in monasteries
and convents to supply refreshment to pilgrims and
travellers. The oldest country house brewery, at Lacock
Abbey in Wiltshire, resulted from the purchase of a nunnery
by William Sharington from Henry VIII. Here, as in other
brewhouses, water heated by the furnace in the bakehouse
next door (from where yeast was supplied), was boiled
and then cooled before being run off into the mash tun
containing barley and malt.

Next, the mixture was stirred for several hours with a
mash paddle to help convert the starch in the cereal into
sugar. The liquid subsequently drawn off was boiled in the
copper with sugar and hops before being drained yet again,
this time into a fermenting tun where yeast was added.

A variety of strengths

In just a few days a good brew was produced which, after
skimming, was either drunk at once or put into casks to
mature further. Generally three strengths were brewed,
a weakish thirst-quencher for everyday consumption
known as beer; a medium strength to accompany family
meals, known as ale and stored in casks, possibly for a year
or more; and a strong brew – malt liquour – for special
occasions, which was invariably bottled.

Other flavoured beers might also be brewed here, including nettle, dandelion and ginger beers. Hops were also used to flavour an unmalted beer, while apples with fermented into cider.

In the malt house

Malting the barley for beer making was done in the winter, possibly in a separate malt house, or by a local miller. Malting involved steeping the grain in water then leaving it to 'sweat' before spreading it out to dry. Hops for flavouring were often grown on the estate. Chamomile flowers were also used for imparting a pleasant taste.

THE LAND STEWARD SHOULD HAVE NO OTHER OCCUPATION OR PROFESSION

NOT LEAST BECAUSE HIS WAS A ROLE OF GREAT RESPONSIBILITY WITHIN THE ESTATE. HE WAS THE TOP MAN UPON WHOM HIS MASTER RELIED ABSOLUTELY.

Any man wishing to fulfil the role of land steward needed to be both versatile and totally reliable. As well as knowledge of agriculture he needed skill in accounting, surveying and architecture, plus the personal accomplishments essential for dealing with 'inferior servants' and with the estate's tenants. The good land steward kept a day book or journal, a ledger, a memorandum book and a general inventory. He also supplied those who worked for him with account books and examined these at regular intervals.

MAKING A SURVEY

The Complete Servant laid out the way in which an initial survey should be made, from which '... *regular memorandums should be made in a book, of every thing necessary to be remarked or executed, of the places where deficiencies are found, or improvements may be made; of buildings and repairs necessary; insurances, dates of leases, rates, nuisances, trespasses, live and dead stock, game, timber, fencing, draining, paths and roads, culture, commons, rivers, and sea coasts, and of every other specific article relative to his trust, which deserves attention, and therefore ought not to be committed to loose papers, or left to memory.'*

Keeping records

The first job of the newly appointed land steward was to survey the estate and make a detailed inventory of everything in it. As each farm on the estate was surveyed, the land steward provided tenants with a copy of their individual map. The steward also needed to keep a record or terrier of all common lands. Any boundary disputes were settled by a jury at the manor court, and also recorded. And to keep a watchful eye on

GATE PIERS: CANONS ASHBY: NORTHANTS

such matters, and on repairs and renovations (including those necessary to roads and bridges), and the like, the conscientious steward rode around the estate daily.

THE GOOD STEWARD

The steward of excellence would also:

• Encourage improvements in cultivation and husbandry, including encouraging tenants to plant orchards.

• Manage woodlands and the planting and felling of trees.

• Look out for the presence of valuable minerals on the estate.

• Let as much of the estate land as possible, and provide leases for tenants.

• Improve the value of the estate, for example by adding roads or facilities such as fisheries.

• Collect rents and make sure that the money is taken to the bank for safe keeping.

CARE OF DEER IS ENTRUSTED TO BOTH PARK-KEEPER AND GAMEKEEPER

A VITAL JOB ON ESTATES WHERE DEER WERE KEPT. REARING PHEASANTS FOR SHOOTING AND SHOOT MANAGEMENT WERE ALSO A KEY PART OF THESE ROLES.

Sound knowledge of the law was essential to the position of gamekeeper. In 1671 an Act was passed which not only granted the right of every landowner to appoint a gamekeeper but allowed him to confiscate dogs, firearms or other 'implements of the chase' from anybody suspected of being unqualified to hunt and to bring any poachers he apprehended to face local justice. The man appointed to the post might also act as

THE PARK-KEEPER'S DUTIES

Summarizing the duties of the park-keeper, Giles Jacob in *The Compleat Sportsman* of 1718 says that he must: *'... daily take turn around his Park, and keep a constant Account of the Number of his Deer; and oftentimes watch them at Night, for their Preservation against unlawful Hunters, especially in Moon-shiny Nights and the Rutting Season. He must take care to calculate an exact Number of Bucks and Does proper to be kill'd in each Season ... and at the same Time not to over-stock the same, preserving a proper number of young Fawns to be bred up in the steads of those he kills...'*

the park-keeper or land steward, or he might be a local tenant farmer or neighbouring estate owner.

Work on estates was often a family affair. In 1885, for example, *The Field* magazine ran advertisements offering gamekeepers themselves and their sons for hire. A keepers' register was also kept at a London gunmaker's. Cottages on the estate were supplied for the park-keeper and if necessary for the head and second gamekeepers.

A job for a woman

Women could be gamekeepers too. One of the best known is Polly Fishburn who served on the estate at Holkham Hall in Norfolk in the early 19th century. This formidable woman, with her short hair cut topped with a man's hat, was renowned for her strength.

THE DAIRYMAID ATTENDS TO THE POULTRY

HER DUTIES ALSO INCLUDED RAISING CHICKS, PLUCKING THEM READY FOR TRUSSING AND MAKING SURE THAT, IN SUMMER, EGGS WERE PRESERVED FOR WINTER USE.

As well as chickens the poultry cared for by the dairymaid included ducks, geese and turkeys and possibly guinea fowl. All were kept in a poultry yard close to the brewhouse or another building producing the warmth that helped the birds to thrive. The dairy maid gathered up the eggs once a day, and needed to be in tune with the ways and needs of her birds, not

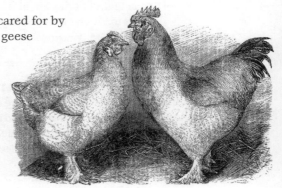

LUXURY ACCOMMODATION

Hen houses were also provided, as colourfully described by Gervase Markham in his *Perfect Husbandry* of 1615 (here in modern spelling): *'Your hen house would be large and spacious with somewhat a high roof and walls strong and windows upon the same rising; round about the inside of the walls upon the ground would be built large pens of 3 ft high for Geese, Ducks and Fowls to sit in.'*

'Near to the eavings …. Would be perches … on which to sit your cocks, hens, capon and turkeys, each on several perches as they are disposed … Let there be pins stuck into the walls so that your poultry may climb to their perches with ease, let the floor be … of earth smooth and easy, let the small fowl have a hole at one end of the house to come in and out at when they please ….'

least because, 'some hens will by cackling tell you when they have layed, but some will lay mute, therefore you must let your own eye be your instruction.'

To help fatten geese and turkeys for good eating, and to keep birds of all kinds laying right through the winter, they were commonly fed malt or mixtures such as oatmeal and treacle and barley meal mashed with milk. If wheat grains were to be given to poultry they first needed to be crushed and soaked in water.

EGG PRESERVATION

To preserve eggs for the winter they were customarily painted with or immersed in gum arabic, dried, then packed into dry charcoal dust. Or they might be kept in a waterglass (sodium silicate) solution. If cooked, they were boiled, shelled and pickled in vinegar.

A HEAD COACHMAN'S OFFICE IS ONE OF CONSIDERABLE TRUST

THIS WAS PARTICULARLY TRUE IN SMALLER HOUSES WHERE THERE WAS NO MASTER OF THE HORSE OR CLERK OF THE STABLES TO WHOM HE HAD TO REPORT.

When in sole charge, the head coachman did not merely drive the family carriages but directed the grooms, postilions and stable hands, order and buy all the hay, corn and other necessities for the horses, and look after the coaches themselves, making sure that they were kept in tip top condition. Knowledge of farriery was also essential.

The daily routine

The head coachman always rose early to supervise the care of the horses. Following breakfast in the house all staff would return to the stable 'shake down the litter on each side of the horses and put the stable in good order, in expectation of their master, who probably, pays them a visit after breakfast to inspect the horses, give orders, or make enquiries.' When mounting the coach the head coachman always took the whip and reins in his left hand and mounted the box on the coach on the near side.

Then followed the cleaning of harnesses and other tack, supervised by the head coachman, and coach cleaning. Each day coaches needed to be washed and the springs, straps and any other leather trappings blacked. The wheels were thoroughly greased and oiled, the insides brushed, glass polished and the lamps cleaned and trimmed.

HORSES AT WORK

Every coachman needed to be good with horses and dextrous with the reins. *'Where two coachman and as many grooms are kept'* said *The Servants' Practical Guide, '... the carriage is probably out three times a day; where one coachman and a groom are kept it is usual to have a carriage out twice only, a pair of horses in the afternoon, and a pair or single horse in the evening, or a pair in the morning and again in the afternoon. A horse for night work is frequently kept when the carriage is much required in the evening, and when the condition of the carriage horses is considered.'*

SPICK AND SPAN

Cleaning tips for coachmen from *The Complete Servant*

Black Dye for Harness: The colour of harness that has become rusty or brown by wear, may be restored to a fine black after the dirt has been sponged and brushed off, by using the following mixture: Boil logwood chips in three quarts of soft water, to which add three ounces of nut-galls [galls from hazels], finely powdered, and one ounce of alum; simmer the whole together for half an hour, and it will be fit for use.

Liquid Blacking for Harness: Take 2 oz. of mutton suet, melted, 6 oz. of purified bees' wax, melted; ¼ lb lamp black; 1 gill of turpentine; 2 oz. of Prussian blue, powdered; 1 oz. of indigo blue, ground; 6 oz. of sugar-candy, melted in a little water; and 2 oz. of soft soap. Mix, and simmer over the fire for 15 minutes, when add a gill of turpentine. Lay it on the harness with a sponge, and then polish it.

THE CHAUFFEUR MUST KEEP HIS CAR IN PROPER CONDITION

WITH THE ARRIVAL OF THE MOTOR CAR THE UNIFORMED CHAUFFEUR BECAME AN ESSENTIAL MEMBER OF THE 'OUTDOOR' COUNTRY HOUSE STAFF.

As motoring gradually took over from the use of carriages and traps in the early part of the 20th century, so chauffeurs replaced coachmen and footmen. Large houses with substantial means might even employ separate chauffeurs for the master and mistress of the house and for other family members. Chauffeurs needed to be expert in all the workings of the motorcar and its repair.

Stable blocks were converted into garages to house

ARISTOCRATIC DRIVERS

Royalty led the way in popularizing motoring. On 29 October 1900 the Duchess of York recorded in her diary her '... *first drive in a motor! To visit Raglan'*. She was accompanied by the Hon. Charles Stewart Rolls who was destined to have his historic meeting with Henry Royce four years later.

vehicles such as the early Daimlers, Rolls Royces and Mercedes, as well as cars such as the Clément-Talbot, first made from imported French parts and developed by the 20th Earl of Shrewsbury and Talbot, a pioneer of motoring, whose principal country residence was at Ingestre Hall in Staffordshire.

MOTORING FOR WOMEN

Women quickly took to motoring – as drivers as well as passengers. *The Lady's Realm* **of 1904, reporting on The Ladies' Automobile Club recorded, for example that the Countess of Kinnoull was** *'an all weather motorist'* **and that***: 'In her 14 h.p. Chenard & Walker car which ranked among her wedding presents she recently motored from her charming Highland home – Dupplin Castle, Perth – to London.'* **On a sartorial note it added:** *'Lady Kinnoull dresses simply and daintily on the car, preferring a three-quarter jackal fur coat for fine and a leather coat for wet weather, a small toque and motor veil, short skirt and thick shoes, which she regards as easier to use than boots for the foot work involved in driving.'*

Ease of travel

Motoring made travelling to and from London and the country easier and more flexible but could play havoc with the tightly knit arrangements of a household. No longer, for instance, did hostesses know to the minute (as printed in railway timetables) exactly when guests would be arriving. And unchaperoned drives were a perfect opportunity for men and women to become intimate.

HOUSES TO VISIT

Key:
NT = National Trust
HHA = Historic Houses Association
EH = English Heritage

All over the country, visitors can experience first hand what country house life was like both above and below stairs. While many of the houses are closed during the winter months, gardens are usually open all year, but it is always wise to check ahead of a visit, and to note any tours or seasonal activities on offer. Those mentioned here were correct at the time of going to press.

A personal selection of outstanding and accessible houses in a wide range of counties are listed here, but check the organizations (in the key above) online for their full lists of houses open for view, and the index of the book for additional suggestions.

(EH) Audley End House in Essex presents brilliant contrasts between decadent Jacobean living quarters, once enjoyed by monarchs James I and Charles II, and a Victorian service wing where visitors can meet the staff. The grounds, landscaped by Capability Brown, boast many neoclassical monuments, a working kitchen garden in which many heritage varieties are grown and stable yard complete with horses.
https://www.english-heritage.org.uk/visit/places/audley-end-house-and-gardens/

(NT) Belton House, Lincolnshire, built in the late 17th century, is a classic country house where as well as fine displays of furniture, porcelain, silver and books, visitors can experience first hand how servants lived and responded to well preserved array of bells below stairs. The boathouse, stables and orangery are among the highlights in the grounds.
https://www.nationaltrust.org.uk/belton-house

(NT) Charlecote Park in Warwickshire is a perfect place to explore Victorian kitchens and the many outbuildings used for a variety of activities. These, and the many family rooms on display, also redesigned in the 19th century, exist in a house dating to the Elizabethan era which still boasts a large hall. The fine and extensive library contains

many Elizabethan works. The surrounding parklands are the work of Capability Brown.
https://www.nationaltrust.org.uk/charlecote-park

(NT) Cragside House in Northumberland was the family home of the inventor and industrialist William Armstrong and the first in the world to be lit by hydroelectricity. His technological wizardry still on display includes telephones, a lift, fire alarm buttons and Turkish baths. The grounds display Armstrong's landscaping abilities, including five lakes, a massive rock garden and millions of trees and shrubs. Models in the Power House allow visitors to generate their own electricity.
https://www.nationaltrust.org.uk/cragside

(NT) Croome Court in Worcestershire is a fine Palladian mansion of the mid 18th century with both house and garden designed by Capability Brown – his first commissioned landscape. Outside, features not to be missed include the glass houses, dipping pond (for collecting water for plants), hot-walled kitchen garden, a Rotunda and garden room. Added to these are statues, temples and a grotto.
https://www.nationaltrust.org.uk/croome

(NT) In the Great Hall of **Dyrham Park** in Gloucestershire visitors can relax and listen to the harpsichord, taking them back to the 18th century. Attached to the baroque-style house is a fine orangery inspired by Versailles and a covered passageway links to a church. A herd of some 200 fallow deer roam the grounds, while the formal gardens include statuary plus artificial lakes and waterfalls.
https://www.nationaltrust.org.uk/dyrham-park

(NT) At **Erdigg Hall** in North Wales the life of servants is vividly brought to life through a collection of ten portraits commissioned from the mid-19th century, each with an accompanying poem. Servants included range from housemaid and butcher to carpenter and gamekeeper. Visitors can also explore the well-equipped kitchen, still room and bakehouse illustrated with practical demonstrations of servant's chores.
http://www.nationaltrust.org.uk/erddig/

(NT) Ham House on the banks of the Thames reveals to its visitors rare insights into the heights of fashion and power in 17th century London in a house packed with superb furniture and textiles that has changed little in 300 years, including 'hands on' servants' quarters. The formal gardens

are also a delight, featuring an ice house, dairy and Britain's oldest orangery.
https://www.nationaltrust.org.uk/ham-house-and-garden

(NT) Hardwick Hall in Derbyshire is an Elizabethan masterpiece built in the late 17th century for Bess of Hardwick, whose story visitors can share. Its architect Robert Smythson also designed nearby **Chatsworth** (also well worth visiting). It boasts a magnificent great hall, many Elizabethan tapestries and a wide variety of family and servants' rooms. Working kitchen gardens are included in the extensive grounds that feature fine herbaceous borders.
https://www.nationaltrust.org.uk/features/discover-the-hall-at-hardwick-

At **Harewood House** in Yorkshire, visitors can open the kitchen cupboards and find them packed with the original utensils and equipment used for creating meals for family and guests. Each weekend the house hosts culinary demonstrations showing exactly how such meals were created, while in the school holidays workshops for children take them back to the era of scullery maids and hall boys who answered the call of the array of bells still displayed below stairs.
http://www.harewood.org/house

Hatfield House, Hertfordshire, has a newly restored Victorian kitchen in the Jacobean house originating to 1611. As well as exploring the work areas, visitors can watch videos showing the roles of chef, kitchen maid, gardener, scullery maid, porter, housekeeper, still room maid and butler of Hatfield House at the time of Queen Victoria's visit in 1846. All the actors are dressed in authentic costumes and their parts played out around the house.
http://www.hatfield-house.co.uk/

(HHA) Highclere Castle in Berkshire is famed as the 'real' Downton Abbey, the chief shooting location for the TV series and the 2019 film. Designed by Charles Barry, and home of the Earl and Countess of Carnarvon, visitors can admire the superbly decorated saloon, dining and drawing rooms as well as the library, music and smoking rooms, staff quarters and cellar. The gardens and grounds, the work of Capability Brown, are also accessible. The *Downton Abbey* tours organized at the house are highly recommended.
https://www.highclerecastle.co.uk/

(NT) Kedleston Hall in Derbyshire is a fine example of how state rooms and family and staff quarters existed separately in the country house. The work of the architect Robert Adam,

many aspects of the house also reflect the design of a Roman villa. Visitors have the chance to see how the house was used in the Edwardian era and, in the gardens, explore the geometric layout that was also Adam's creation.
https://www.nationaltrust.org.uk/kedleston-hall

(NT) Kingston Lacy in Dorset is a lavish family home built and decorated to resemble an Italian palace. As well as its many fine rooms containing art (notably in the Spanish room) and antiquities, are the library and state bedrooms. Visitors can also see the 'tented' bachelor quarters and kitchens. The notable fine gardens contain an Egyptian obelisk, and a Victorian fernery.
https://www.nationaltrust.org.uk/kingston-lacy

(NT) Knightshayes Court in Devon is a superb example of a high Victorian gothic country house. With hall, morning room, drawing room, smoking and billiard rooms all on display it is easy to see how the house worked for both family and servants. The gardens also have much to admire including terraces, topiary, herbaceous borders, woodland and a walled kitchen garden.
https://www.nationaltrust.org.uk/knightshayes

(NT) At **Lanhydrock** in Cornwall, essentially a family home, the Victorian kitchen adjoining rooms including laundry and bakehouse can be experienced, complete with their equipment. Also on view are the contrasting elegant drawing and dining rooms and the sparse servants' bedrooms and nurseries. Visitors can take the roles of kitchen maids and footmen (complete with livery) and carry out tasks ranging from jam making to attending to brushing down clothes.
http://www.nationaltrust.org.uk/lanhydrock/

(NT) Montacute House in Somerset is a masterpiece of Elizabethan Renaissance architecture where visitors can explore the life and times of its original Tudor inhabitants and their successors. Many rooms, including the magnificent long gallery are open for view, including some bedrooms and are used to display a range of portraits belonging to the National Portrait Gallery. The daily guided tour is recommended.
https://www.nationaltrust.org.uk/montacute-house

Penshurst Place in Kent is a privately owned 14th century house, once the property of Henry VIII, remarkable for its unique Baron's hall. The beautifully furnished state rooms,

dining room, tapestry room and galleries all evidence the lives lived within its walls. The gardens are still arranged in the Tudor style leading to extensive parklands.
https://www.penshurstplace.com

(NT) Visit **Polesden Lacy** in Surrey and explore the life of the Edwardian socialite Margaret Greville who with her husband updated the Victorian house and filled it with fine furniture, art, porcelain and silver. More and more parts of the house are opened each year, and now include servants' quarters. The themed visitor tours of the house are recommended.
https://www.nationaltrust.org.uk/polesden-lacey

(NT) In Wiltshire, **Stourhead's** 18th century Palladian mansion, offers the chance to see clearly how a country house operated both above and below stairs for the benefit of the family and its employees. For the best 'behind the scenes' experience, book one of the special tours on offer. The gardens are deservedly famous for its lake and monuments (notably the Pantheon) sited to create spectacular views.
https://www.nationaltrust.org.uk/stourhead

(NT) **Tatton Park** in Cheshire provides the chance to explore a 19th-century neoclassical mansion, including drawing and music rooms, a superb library of over 8,000 books, many of which can now be accessed digitally on request. The scullery, salting room and wine cellar all help to reveal what life was like for the servants. The deer park, farm and gardens, including a fernery and Japanese garden, all add to the country house experience.
https://www.nationaltrust.org.uk/tatton-park

(NT) The **Uppark** house of today is a faithful restoration of the 17th century West Sussex house severely fire damaged in 1989. Furniture, pictures and chandeliers from the 18th century can be appreciated, plus the servants' quarters, joined to the main building by tunnels. These include a hall, still room, scullery and butler's and housekeeper's rooms. There is a fine set of bells and an extensive cellar. The gardens were landscaped by Humphrey Repton.
https://www.nationaltrust.org.uk/uppark-house-and-garden

BOOK REFERENCE LIST

THE FOLLOWING ARE THE MAJOR SOURCES OF
QUOTATIONS INCLUDED IN THE BOOK.

*Cassell's Household Guide, A Guide
to Every Department of Practical Life,
volumes 1 – 4*, published in the 1880s
by Cassell Peter & Galpin.

*Complete Etiquette for Ladies and
Gentlemen:* A guide to the observances
of good society. Published by Ward,
Lock & Company, 1900.

Enquire Within of 1894, published by
Houlston and Sons.

Home Chat, bind up of issues from
March 12 to June 13, 1896. Published
by the Harmsworth Press.

Life in the Victorian Kitchen, 2014,
Karen Foy, published by Pen & Sword
History.

Mrs A.B. Marshall's Book of Cookery,
published by Ward, Lock & Company,
1888.

*Mrs Beeton's Book of Household
Management*, original edition
published by S.O. Beeton Publishing.

*Our Homes and How to Make Them
Healthy*, edited by Shirley Forster
Murphy, 1883. Facsimile edition 2015
published by Sagwan Press.

The Complete Servant of 1675, Hannah
Woolley. Also the 1825 edition by
Samuel Adams (servant) and Sarah
Adams. Published by Knight and Lacy.

The English Flower Garden, 1883,
William Robinson, published by John
Murray.

The Formal Garden in England,
Reginald Blomfield. Published by
Macmillan and Co., Limited, 1901.

The Gardener's Assistant, 1859, Robert
Thompson, published by Blackie and
Son.

The Lady's Realm, a selection of the
monthly issues: November 1904 to
April 1905. Published by Arrow Books
Ltd, 1972.

The Servants Book of Knowledge,
Anthony Heasel. Published by J.
Cooke, at Shakespear's-Head, Pater-
noster Row, 1773.

The Servants' Practical Guide of 1880,
an unknown author. Subtitled 'a
handbook of duties and rules'.
Published by Frederick Warne.

INDEX

OTHER GREAT TITLES FROM RYDON PUBLISHING

Weeds on Trial
Ruth Binney
ISBN: 978-1910821-27-5

Animal Lore and Legend
Ruth Binney
ISBN: 978-1-910821-15-2

The No.1 Book of Numbers
Ruth Binney
ISBN: 978-1-910821-17-6

Plant Lore and Legend
Ruth Binney
ISBN: 978-1-910821-10-7

THE AUTHOR
Ruth Binney holds a degree in Natural Sciences from Cambridge University and has been involved in countless publications during her career as an editor. She is the author of many successful natural history and nostalgia titles. She lives in Somerset.
www.ruthbinney.com

PICTURE CREDITS
Page 3, 4, 5, 7, 24, 38, 41, 43, 61, 73, 77, 92, 143, 146, 149, 156, 157, 166, 167, 169, 172, 174, 198, 208 courtesy British Library Flickr collection.
Page 25, 58 Trade Catalogue of Young & Marten, first published 1895.
Where no copyright information is available, every effort has been made to trace copyright holders and obtain permission to reproduce this material.

www.rydonpublishing.co.uk